23~10~85

BIBLE CLASS COMMENTARY

BIBLE CLASS COMMENTARY

1 & 2 CORINTHIANS

Henry T. Mahan

 EVANGELICAL PRESS

EVANGELICAL PRESS
16—18 High Street, Welwyn, Herts, AL6 9EQ, England.

First published 1985

ISBN 0 85234 194 6

Cover picture: The ancient ruins at Corinth, photographed
from the centre of the Agora looking over the
ruins of the Northwest Shops towards the
Temple of Appolo.
By kind permission of Rev. R. Simpson.

Typeset in Great Britain by Beaver Reprographics,
Watford, Hertfordshire.
Printed by Anchor Brendon, Tiptree, Essex.

CONTENTS

1 CORINTHIANS

To the church of God at Corinth

1 Corinthians 1 : 1-9

Paul taught in Corinth for a year and a half (Acts 18:1, 11). He left Corinth and sailed to Syria. During his absence false teachers crept in and disturbed the church with false doctrine and unscriptural practices. The church fell into factions and divisions and misuse of gifts. Questions arose about marriage and going to law with one another. The resurrection was doubted by some, and the ordinances were abused. They flaunted their learning, grew careless in their conduct and purity of doctrine began to decline! This epistle deals with these issues and many more problems confronting this young church.

vv. 1, 2.   We have the usual salutation or inscription. The writer describes himself by his name and his office: **'Paul, called to be an apostle'**. His call to the apostleship was **'by the will of God'**. No one ought to take such an office or responsibility unless he is called and appointed to it by God (1 Tim. 1:12; Acts 9:15). Sosthenes was the ruler of the Jewish synagogue at Corinth. Luke mentions him in Acts 18:17. Evidently he had been converted and was with Paul, for Paul calls him his brother.

The epistle is addressed to **'the church of God . . . at Corinth'** — a congregation of believers joined together in fellowship, worship and the preaching of the gospel. Paul's letter is intended for those who are **'sanctified in Christ Jesus'**, set apart from all eternity to grace and glory and justified by the blood and righteousness of Christ (Heb. 10:10-14). Not only are they chosen and justified, but they are **'called to be saints'**. They are called by his Spirit and by his Word to repentance toward God and faith in the Lord Jesus. The

epistle is intended for all other believers, in all places, who call
upon the name of the Lord Jesus! Paul says, 'Christ is my Lord
and their Lord!'

v.3.   Nothing is more desirable than to have God reconciled
to us through Christ, and this is signified by the word **'grace'**.
Then to have peace with God, peace of heart and conscience
and peace among ourselves, even in a world of trial and trouble,
is indeed the greatest blessing. The foundation of all grace and
peace is the favour of God through the merits of Christ.

v.4.   **'I always'** (as often as he thought of them) **'thank God
for you and for the grace of God given to you by Christ.'** This
includes all sorts of grace (electing, justifying, regenerating and
sanctifying grace) and every grace of the Spirit (as repentance,
faith, hope, love, etc.); for all are the gifts of God in them
(1 Thess. 2:13). No work nor gift of grace is by man's free will
or merit, but all are owing to God's grace and come through
the hands of Christ (1 Cor. 4:7).

v.5.   This is a continuation of the thanksgiving. 'In Christ in
every respect you are enriched and provided for.' Not only did
they have a spiritual, experimental knowledge of the gospel of
Christ, but many of them had been richly qualified with gifts
to preach and teach the gospel. Some had the gift to speak in
other tongues and other gifts of the Spirit.

v.6.   By the **'testimony of Christ'** is meant the gospel (2 Tim.
1:8). This gospel had been preached to the Corinthians and
was confirmed and established among them by the signs and
miracles with which it was attended and by the Holy Spirit's
applying it to their hearts (Heb. 2:1-4).

v.7.   The Corinthians were not only honoured with the light
of the gospel, but God endowed them with many gifts and
graces so that they were not inferior to any of the churches.
However, Paul does not ascribe unto them such abundance as
to leave nothing to be desired, but merely as much as will

suffice until Christ comes and they shall be made perfect (1 John 3:1, 2; 1 Thess. 1:9, 10).

v. 8.   Paul lets them know what hope he has of them as to the future. 'The Lord will never forsake you but will complete what he has begun in you' (Phil. 1:6). The love of God to his people always continues. Their interest in Christ will never be lost. Grace in them is eternal life, and they will never totally be moved away from the hope of the gospel. In the day of our Lord Jesus every believer will be presented blameless, not in themselves, for no man is without fault and sin; but in Christ's righteousness all the elect are blameless, being justified by his blood and clothed in his righteousness (Col. 1:20-22; Eph. 1:3,4; Jude 24, 25).

v. 9.   When the Scriptures speak of God as **'faithful'**, the meaning in many cases (and here especially) is that what God purposes and promises, he provides. He shall not fail (Rom. 11:29; Mal. 3:6). 'He has called you into the companionship and fellowship of his Son, and he will faithfully discharge every promise to Christ and to you' (John 6:37-39; 10:27-29; Rom. 4:20-25).

Let there be no divisions among you

1 Corinthians 1 : 10-18

v. 10.   Up to this point Paul had handled these Corinthians mildly; now he begins to deal with some of the problems that existed among them. **'I urge you and appeal to you by the name of the Lord Jesus Christ.'** That name must have had weight and influence among them, for it is by his name they were called, justified and accepted by the Father. Christ is precious to every believer, and it was his honour and interest which was at stake by their divisions and errors. Paul was not

acting in his own name, nor seeking to preserve his reputation
as a preacher, but he was concerned for the glory of Christ and
the testimony of the gospel (1 Tim. 6:1; Titus 2:5; Phil.
3:17, 18).

The apostle exhorts three things:

1. *'Speak the same things.* Profess the same truths and
preach the same message of grace in Christ.'

2. *'Have no divisions* and quarrelling among you.' Nothing
is more inconsistent on the part of believers than to be at odds
with one another.

3. *'Live in harmony together'.* The foundation of harmony
is for all to be agreed in mind and judgement, not only on
matters of doctrine, but on other matters also.

v.11.   Chloe was evidently a woman member of the church
whose husband was dead, for Paul refers to the household by
her name. They were probably a family of great influence and
integrity in the church and had written to Paul concerning the
problems in this church. Paul says, 'My information comes
from a good source.'

v.12.   Some of the church members were divided into
factions. One group said, 'We are of Paul. He was instrumental
in our conversion. We like his way of teaching. He is our
pattern; we won't hear anyone else.' Another group said,
'We don't care for Paul; we like Apollos,' while another
claimed Peter as their champion. Still others said, 'We are of
Christ; we don't need the pastors and teachers at all.'

v.13.   The body of Christ is not to be divided! He is our Lord
and Master; he was crucified for us and we were baptized in his
name, not in the name of his ministers. We are all one in Christ
(Gal. 3:26-28). The minister has his gifts, as all others have
theirs, and one is not to be exalted above the other (1 Cor.
12:12-20).

vv.14-16.   The apostle did not dislike the ordinance of
baptism, nor was he discounting its value or importance, but

because he was an apostle and was held in great esteem for his faith and his gifts, he was thankful that he personally baptized so few, lest he be charged with having a personal following, or lest people whom he baptized find some cause for pride or comfort in the fact that they were baptized by Paul himself!

v.17.   He anticipates an objection that he was neglecting the Lord's command to 'go and teach all nations, baptizing them'. So he says, 'Baptism is not the chief and principal business of the ministers, but their main business is to preach the gospel of Christ!' (1 Cor. 2:2; 9:16; Gal. 6:14.)   And that preaching of the gospel was not with man's wisdom, human eloquence and oratory, or in a show of vanity and false piety, but in a plain, humble and modest manner. The method of preaching which he pursued was the opposite of show and ambition; it was very simple and to the point, for which the false teachers despised him. When men's ears and minds are tickled and entertained by our human wisdom and eloquence, the gospel of Christ is pushed aside, and nothing remains but dead theology. The issues are clouded, the simplicity of Christ is misunderstood and the faith of our hearers stands in our wisdom, not in the person and power of Christ (2 Cor. 11:3; 1 Cor. 2:4, 5).

v.18.   The preaching of salvation by the grace of God alone by the crucified Christ, the preaching of righteousness, peace and reconciliation by the blood of his cross, the preaching of a sufficient sacrifice and atonement by Christ offering up himself on the cross in our room and stead is sheer nonsense to those who are perishing, whether they are in the church or the world. But unto us who are being saved by the power and grace of God, this gospel is both the power of salvation and a revelation of the wisdom of God. We see in Christ crucified our deliverance from the curse of the law, and we see in Christ crucified how God can be both just and Justifier of those who believe (Rom. 8:1,33,34; 3:19-26).

He that glorieth, let him glory in the Lord

1 Corinthians 1 : 19-31

In verse 18 Paul declares that the preaching of the gospel of Christ is foolishness to natural men. The mysteries of grace are hidden from the wise and prudent (Matt. 11:25; 1 Cor. 2:7, 8). So it is nothing unusual for men who are distinguished for wisdom in other areas to reject totally and despise the gospel of redemption.

v. 19.   In a quotation from Isaiah 29:14, Paul shows how unreasonable it is to question the gospel of the cross on the ground that the so-called wise men of the world call it foolishness. God says, 'I will render useless their wisdom, learning and philosophy.' Men who are wise in their own esteem become fools, men who profess to see by the light of human wisdom are struck blind and the wisdom of this world becomes vain and worthless when it exalts itself against God (2 Thess. 2:10-12; 1 Cor. 3:18).

v. 20.   Where is the wise man, who boasts of his superior wisdom and knowledge? Where are the scribe and the scholar? Where is the debater and disputer of this world, who derives his wisdom, not from the Holy Spirit, but from human understanding? They are not to be found among those whom the Lord uses to minister the gospel, to write the Scriptures, or to lead his church. Without Christ all sciences are vain, all roads lead to ruin and all human wisdom is foolishness. The gospel exposes all worldly wisdom to be what it is — foolishness (Rom. 1:18-24).

v. 21.   When the world (with all of its earthly wisdom) failed to recognize and know the living God by means of its own philosophy, God (in his wisdom and purpose) was pleased to reveal himself and his salvation (purchased and provided by Christ) through the very means the world calls foolishness — the preaching of the gospel! While the wise men of the world are left to perish in their sins (ignorant of God), the gospel they despise has become the power of God unto salvation to all that believe in Christ (Rom. 1:14-17).

v. 22.   The Jews required a sign from heaven that Christ is the Messiah. Though miracles were wrought and Scriptures fulfilled, they required their own signs in their own way. The Greeks (those distinguished by superior intelligence) seek after that which satisfies human intellect.

v. 23.   We preach a crucified Christ, bearing our sins in his body on the tree, forsaken of God and rejected of men. To the Jew this message is a scandal and an offensive stumbling-block, and to the Greek it is sheer nonsense and absurd.

vv. 24, 25.   But to those who are called, enlightened and taught of God, Christ crucified is not only **'the power of God'** to save, but **'the wisdom of God'**. We see in Christ the law honoured, justice satisfied and every attribute of God glorified, enabling him to be just and Justifier (Rom. 3:19-26). What men call foolish (if it is of God) is wiser than men, and what men call weakness (if it is of God) is stronger than men.

vv. 26-28.   'Consider your own calling; look about you in the church. Not many of you' (he does not say *none* of the noble and mighty are called, for some were saved) 'were considered to be wise according to human standards; not many of you were influential, powerful, or of a high and noble birth. But God chose those whom the world calls foolish to put the wise to shame. God chose the weak to put the strong to shame. God deliberately chose the low-born and those branded with contempt, even those looked upon as nothing, that he might bring to nothing the high.'

v.29. God's purpose in choosing and calling these is to banish for ever any glorying in the flesh, that no man may attribute his salvation to anything in himself, but wholly to the sovereign grace and good pleasure of God. There is nothing left us in which we may glory in his presence.

v.30. It is not of us but totally from God that we are in Christ and that we have life in Christ. Christ is our **'wisdom'**, revealing to us the mysteries of godliness and spiritual truth. Christ is our **'righteousness'** making us upright, and putting us in right standing with God. Christ is our **'sanctification'**, making us pure, holy and unblameable. Christ is our **'redemption'**, providing our ransom from the curse and condemnation of sin.

v.31. So then it is written: **'He that** boasts, rejoices and **glories, let him glory** only **in the Lord!'** (Jer. 9:23, 24.)

Faith not in wisdom of men but in power of God

1 Corinthians 2 : 1-8

Paul, in this chapter, continues to teach that the gospel does not need the wisdom of men. It is far above the wisdom of men, it is made known to men only by the Spirit of God and it can only be known and discerned by spiritual men (vv.14, 15).

v.1. 'When I came to Corinth to preach the unsearchable riches of Christ' (the gospel, which is called **'the testimony of God'** because it bears a testimony to his love, grace and mercy in giving his beloved Son to be our Saviour and Redeemer), 'I did not preach this message in lofty words of eloquence, or human philosophy, or man's wisdom' (Acts 18:5).

v. 2. Though Paul was well educated in Jewish learning, had a good knowledge of Greek literature and was capable of conversing with almost anyone on current thoughts and issues, he was resolved to make nothing the subject of his ministry and message **'save Jesus Christ, and him crucified'.** That which was the greatest offence to others was the most delightful thing to him because salvation comes only through and by the obedience and death of Christ (Gal. 6:14; 2:20, 21).

v. 3. By **'weakness'** Paul may mean his bodily presence (2 Cor. 10:10; 12:7-9) or his humble and lowly existence among them, for he worked with his hands to minister to his necessities (Acts 18:3), not exerting his office nor authority as an apostle of Christ (2 Cor. 11:5-9; 1 Cor. 9:1-14). By **'fear and trembling'** I doubt that the apostle meant that he was afraid of what men would do to him, though I am sure he was concerned about the violence and persecution that threatened his life (Acts 18:9-11). It may be that he refers to the greatness and awfulness of the ministry in which he was engaged. He was deeply concerned that he preach the truth of God and that men receive the truth (Rom. 9:1-3; 10:1).

v. 4. As Paul determined, so he acted! His subject matter was not nature, arts, sciences, philosophy, nor dry morality, but salvation from sin through the crucified Christ. So his style of preaching, his language and his messages were delivered, not in human logic, wisdom and persuasion, but in the power and demonstration of the Holy Spirit (John 6:44, 45). It is not by human wisdom, wit, or will that the gospel is believed and received, but by the regeneration and revelation of the Holy Spirit (John 3:3, 5; 1:12, 13; Matt. 16:15-17).

v. 5. This is the key statement — the conclusion of the whole matter. Paul knew that conviction of sin, a revelation of Christ crucified, risen and enthroned, saving faith in Christ alone (apart from merit or works) and a living, vital union with Christ are heart works performed in individuals by the power of God. When this work is accomplished by his Spirit and by

his power, the confidence and assurance of the believer are not
in the preacher, nor in his persuasion, nor in his personality,
but in Christ alone (Phil. 3:3).

vv.6, 7. 'But lest you think that the gospel of Christ is
unworthy of regard and notice because of the simplicity of it
or the lowliness of its ministers and its followers, I declare that
the gospel of the crucified Redeemer is the highest wisdom a
man can imagine. It is the very **wisdom of God**, and those who
are mature in faith recognize it as such.' This gospel is not the
philosophy, plan and wisdom of this world, nor of the leaders
and rulers of this world (which wisdom is foolishness and will
mean nothing); but it is the setting forth of the eternal wisdom,
grace and mercy of God, which was given us in Christ before
the world began. This redemptive plan was hidden in promises,
prophecies and types, but is now revealed in Christ (Heb. 1:1-5).

v.8. None of this world's rulers, religious leaders, nor philosophers saw the wisdom of God in Christ, or they would never
have crucified the Lord of glory. There is no neutral state
regarding the person and work of Christ. It is either foolishness,
or it is the wisdom and power of God! (1 Cor. 1:18; Matt.
12:30.)

Spiritual discernment

1 Corinthians 2 : 9-16

v.9. This is a quotation from Isaiah 64:4 to prove that the
gospel of Christ is mysterious and hidden wisdom, unknown to
the wise and prudent of this world. This is not speaking of the
happiness of heaven, but of the blessings and benefits of Christ,
as the context shows. Though God's mercy to sinners in Christ
is to be seen, read in Scripture and heard by preaching, the
eye, ear and heart of natural man can neither see, hear, nor

understand it (John 3:3; Matt. 13:13-16). The gospel must be
revealed (1 John 5:20).

v.10.   Since the gospel is unknown to natural men (it is
beyond the understanding of the wisest of them), how can any
be acquainted with· these spiritual mysteries? The answer is
here in this verse. God has made a revelation of his purpose to
save, of the person and work of Christ, and of how he can be
just and Justifier by his Spirit (John 16:8-15). Our Quickener,
Teacher and Comforter, the Holy Spirit, has a complete and
perfect knowledge of everything that is, or belongs to, the
gospel of Christ (Eph. 3:8-11).

v.11.   'What person knows and understands what passes
through a man's thoughts except the man's own spirit within
him?' A man's designs, purposes and intentions can never be
known by another man unless the man's own spirit reveals
them. Even so, the eternal purpose of God, the hidden wisdom
of God and the mysteries of his love in Christ are known by no
man. But the Spirit of God knows the thoughts of his heart,
his purposes, will, ways and decrees.

v.12.   'We have not received the carnal spirit which belongs
to this world (that is, the carnal wisdom, philosophy and
thoughts of natural men, which lie in the wisdom of worldly
things and follow them for worldly advantage); but we have
been given by God, and have received, the Holy Spirit of God'
(1 Cor. 1:19-21). He is the Spirit of truth, of illumination,
of adoption and of comfort, and he is the seal and earnest of
future glory. 'God has given us his Spirit of truth that we may
know, understand and appreciate the gifts of his divine favour
and blessings so freely given to us by God in Christ Jesus'
(Eph. 1:16-20; 1 John 1:1-4; Matt. 16:15-17).

v.13.   'And we are setting forth these truths in our preaching,
not in words learned in the schools of philosophers or with the
logic taught and understood by natural men, but we preach
and teach the gospel in the language of the Scripture written

by the Spirit of God. We interpret spiritual truth in spiritual
language to spiritual people. The best interpreter of Scripture
is Scripture (2 Peter 1:20, 21; 2 Tim. 3:16, 17). We compare
the New Testament with the Old Testament, and their truth
and harmony are seen (Luke 24:44-46; Acts 10:43).

v.14.   The natural, unregenerate man (whether in the world
or in the church) will not receive, understand, nor believe in
his heart these truths of God and the revelation of the Spirit of
God. The gospel of grace, of a crucified Redeemer, is sheer
nonsense to him. He is incapable of understanding these
mysteries of God because they are understood in a spiritual
manner, by spiritual light and by the revelation of the Holy
Spirit. As there must be natural faculties to understand natural
things, so there must be spiritual faculties to understand
spiritual truth.

v.15.   'He that is spiritual' includes every person who is born
of the Spirit of God, breathes after spiritual things and has a
saving interest in Christ. He discerns, not all things natural or
all things spiritual (there are many things he does not know),
but all things necessary to faith and salvation. These truths of
sin, sovereignty, substitution and satisfaction in Christ are
plain to him. The spiritual man himself is not understood by
natural men. They do not know who he is, what he is, or why
he believes as he does (John 15:17-21).

v.16.   'Who has known the deep counsels of God? Who
knows the purpose of salvation in Christ? Who knows the
hidden mysteries in the types and shadows of the Old Testament that he may instruct this spiritual man? It is certainly
not the philosophers or the wise men of this world. But we
apostles are abundantly qualified to instruct him, for we have
the mind of Christ' (Eph. 4:11-15).

God gave the increase

1 Corinthians 3 : 1-9

In chapter 3 Paul returns to the subject of divisions and problems in the church, which was the occasion for this epistle.

v.1.   Quite frankly, Paul is saying to the Corinthian brethren (he softens the harshness of his rebuke by calling them **'brethren'**), 'I have not been able to talk to you as I would talk to mature, spiritual men and women because you are indicating by your attitude and behaviour that you are mere infants in the faith. More than that, you are acting like natural, worldly people. You behave as non-spiritual men of flesh in whom the carnal nature predominates.' Sometimes the term **'babes in Christ'** is taken in a good sense (1 Peter 2:2; Luke 18:17). Here it is not good, for it refers to the understanding and the attitude (1 Cor. 14:20).

v.2.   Paul refers more to the *manner* and *form* of his teaching than to the *substance* of the doctrine, for Christ is both milk to babes and strong meat to those of full age. But there is a growth in grace and in the knowledge of Christ which was hindered by their attitude and carnality. The wise teacher begins with the first principles of Christ and moves higher in the mysteries and wisdom of Christ as the hearer is able to follow (Mark 4:33; John 16:12). The gospel of Christ contains everything necessary to be known. Spiritual growth enables a person to drink deeper, comprehend more of the riches of Christ and mature in faith and conduct. We don't have one message for young believers and another for elders. The elders are able to see and understand more of the riches in Christ because of their maturity. This was the Corinthian problem — growth impeded by carnality and childishness.

v. 3. To prove that the carnal nature prevailed in them and that they were not spiritually mature believers, Paul calls attention to their **'envy, strife and divisions'**. These are fruits of the flesh and, where they prevail, it is evident that the partakers are not spiritual but carnal! (Gal. 5:22.) 'You are behaving like unregenerate men.' From envy comes strife, and strife leads to open divisions and factions.

v. 4. Paul specifies the particular form of division. One group was a fan club for Paul and set him up as their master above all others. Others said, 'We prefer Apollos; we don't care for Paul.' Some preferred Peter (1 Cor. 1:12), while others rejected all ministers and claimed only to be followers of Christ. 'Is not this a demonstration of carnality and flesh?'

v. 5. **'Who is Paul? Who is Apollos?** What are they? They are only ministering servants of the Lord Jesus through whom you heard the gospel.' They are not masters, nor party heads, nor lords! They are only instruments in the hands of the Master to feed his flock (Matt. 23:8-12). The pastors are to be respected, heeded and followed as they follow Christ, but they are not to be sources of contention, nor are they to lord it over God's heritage (Heb. 13:17; 1 Peter 5:1-5).

v. 6. If the earth is to bring forth fruit, there is need of ploughing, planting and watering. But after all this is done, our labour would be in vain unless the Lord from heaven gives the increase by giving life through the sun and by his secret influence. In like manner, the Word of God is the seed. His faithful servants plough, plant and water, but life is the miracle of divine grace! He who has received the seed has need of watering until full maturity is reached. Apollos, then, who succeeded Paul in the ministry of Corinth, is said to have watered what Paul had sown.

v. 7. **'So neither is he who plants anything** special, **nor he who waters, but** only **God,** who makes it live, grow and become greater.' Ministers of the Word are labourers together

with God, ministers of Christ and stewards of the grace of
God, and are to be loved, respected and heard. But they are
nothing in themselves! They have nothing except what they
have received. All their gifts are from God. Nothing is to be
ascribed to them directly, but all glory is to our Lord (1 Cor.
1:31).

v. 8. The planter and the waterer are one. They preach one
gospel. Their views, aims and end (which are the glory of God
and the good of the church) are one! They have the same love
and affections for one another, so there is no reason for the
church to be divided over them.

'**Every man will receive his own reward according to his
labour.**' While the servants' labours are different, their goal is
the same — not to catch the applause and approval of the
world, but to please and glorify the Lord. This is not a reward
of debt (for our labours are by no means meritorious) but to
hear him say, 'Well done, thou good and faithful servant.'

v. 9. This sums up what has gone before and is the best
argument of all. 'We are all fellow-labourers, fellow-workmen
and joint-promoters with and for God. It is the Lord's work in
which we are employed, and it is to him we devote ourselves
and our service. You are God's garden, field and vineyard
under cultivation; you are God's building. We ministers are but
his labourers' (Isa. 60:21).

Ministers of the gospel exhorted

1 Corinthians 3 : 10-23

It is quite obvious that most of what is written in these verses
is directed to, or talking about, those who minister the gospel.

v. 10. Paul attributes his gifts, his usefulness and his success

as a labourer and builder in the church to 'the grace of God'
(1 Cor. 15:10). Ministers are instruments God makes use of,
and they labour in vain unless the Lord builds the house
(Ps. 127:1). Paul calls himself 'a wise masterbuilder' in respect
to the foolish false teachers and because he was the chief
apostle to the Gentiles. 'The foundation' he laid is Christ (his
person and work), and he warns those ministers who follow
him to be careful how they carry on the work of building on '
this foundation.

v. 11.   This statement consists of two parts. First, *Christ is
the only foundation of the church.* Second, *this Corinthian
church had been rightly founded upon Christ* through Paul's
preaching (1 Cor. 1:23, 24; 2:1-5). Christ alone is our righteousness, redemption, sanctification, wisdom and satisfaction
for life and glory (Eph. 2:19-21). Any other foundation is
sand and will perish (Isa. 28:16).

v. 12.   Paul and the apostles have laid the foundation, which
is Christ. Those ministers who follow (preaching the gospel of
his grace, the valuable truths of the gospel which agree with
the foundation) are said to build lasting and permanent fruits,
such as gold, silver and precious stones. The fruit of their
ministry will stand the test of time and the fires of judgement.
Other ministers' works are compared to wood, hay and stubble,
which can survive neither time nor fire. It is doubtful that Paul
refers to heretical doctrine, denial of Christ, or another gospel
which would overturn the foundation, but these ministers,
while professing Christ, preach empty, useless and trifling
things, such as philosophy, intellectualism, form, ceremony
and traditions. Without any bad design, through education,
ambition or ignorance, these elements may find their way into
a man's ministry and produce bad results.

v. 13.   The doctrine a man preaches and the fruits of his
ministry will sooner or later be made manifest to himself and
to his hearers, who shall clearly see the deformity of the
building and the false hope created by these fleshly efforts.

Certainly the Day of Judgement will reveal the false and the true, but some believe that Paul is saying that in this world, before the great day of the Lord, true hope and true union with Christ, as opposed to false profession, will be revealed. By 'fire' is meant, not the destruction of the world and all evil, but the fire of trial, affliction and testing, which is for a revelation of true faith (James 1:2, 3). If a man is a true minister of the gospel, before the end of his life, he and his hearers will know whether what they have built on Christ, the foundation, is lasting, precious material or wood, hay and stubble.

v.14. If a minister's work and doctrine will bear the test of the Word, the test of time and the test of trial and affliction, it will shine all the brighter for being tried and he will receive the reward of personal joy, the gratitude of those to whom he ministered and the praise of Christ, who will say, 'Well done, good and faithful servant.'

v.15. If a minister's labour and work crumble about him and prove to be false professions and useless human religion, he shall suffer the loss of all labour, efforts and praise which he received from man. He will see the folly of whatever drew him into the way of preaching. But he, himself, shall be saved (notwithstanding all the imperfections of his ministry) upon the foundation of Christ. He will be like a man burned out of house and home; he escapes with his own life but loses all about him.

vv.16, 17. The church is '**the temple of God**'. God dwells in them and with them. '**If any man** by the wisdom of the world (through philosophy, vain deceit, bringing in false doctrines and heresies) **corrupt** their minds from the simplicity of Christ, and make divisions among them, **him shall God destroy**, body and soul, in hell.' God's church is holy, or sacred to him. He will not hold him guiltless who defiles it with error.

vv.18-20. Here Paul puts his finger on the true sore! The

whole mischief originated in this — preachers and people were
wise in their own conceit. Carnal and worldly wisdom must be
discarded as dull and foolish. For a man to be wise in a spiritual
sense, he must be convinced of his own sinfulness, folly and
inability, and must embrace the gospel of Christ, which is
foolishness to this world and despised by men. He must deny
his worldly wisdom and his righteous self and wholly rest and
rely on Christ (Jer. 9:23, 24).

vv. 21-23.   The apostle goes back to the beginning of this
theme (1 Cor. 3:3, 4). 'Let no man glory in ministers, who
(even the best of them), are but men. All ministers and all they
are endowed with are for your benefit and advantage and for
God's glory. All things are for your good and your eternal
salvation (Rom. 8:28-31). All that God does in and with this
world is for your sake. Life, death, things present and things to
come are designed to make you like Christ, because you are
Christ's and he is God's Beloved, Anointed and Heir, in whom
God has vested all things.'

Stewards of the grace of God

1 Corinthians 4 : 1-8

It was a matter of grave concern to Paul to see the church torn
by factions because of liking or disliking certain ministers, so
he continues his discussion as to the ministry of the Word.
Four things are especially prominent:
    1. Paul describes the office of a pastor.
    2. He sets forth the duty of a pastor.
    3. He calls all servants of Christ before the only true
judgement-seat.
    4. He ascribes every gift to the grace of God.

v. 1.   Let pastors and teachers be looked upon as ministering

servants of Christ — qualified, called and sent forth by him to
preach his gospel. Since they are his servants (his ambassadors),
they are to apply themselves to his work, not their own!
(2 Cor. 5:18-21.) Since they are servants, they are to be
respected, esteemed and heard for his sake. When ministers are
treated with contempt, contempt for the Word of God follows;
but when they are exalted above measure, they are in danger
of abusing the office.

These ministers are 'stewards' (a person put in charge of the
affairs of an estate) 'of the mysteries', or the secret purposes,
'of God'. It is their business to dispense and make known the
mysteries of divine grace. Through them God communicates to
men his Word, his gospel, and the directions for his church
(Acts 8:30, 31; Eph. 4:11-15).

v. 2.   It is not enough for a pastor to fill an office, undertake
the duties of the ministry, or be a steward, if he is not a good
and faithful servant — faithful to God's Word, to the gospel
and to those under his care (Acts 20:18-21, 24-27). Everyone
who knows and preaches the truth is not necessarily faithful,
but only he who studies, prays, labours and gives his whole
heart and life to this glorious calling.

v. 3.   Paul knew his call to the apostleship (1 Tim. 1:12, 13;
1 Cor. 1:1). He examined his own heart, ways and motives,
and determined that he had indeed been faithful to his charge
(2 Tim. 4:5-8). Therefore, it mattered very little to him
personally that these Corinthians should judge him and his
ministry. He chose not to stand or fall by their judgement,
nor by any other human judgement (even his own).

v. 4.   Staying with the context, which is 'faithful in the
ministry of the Word', Paul says, '**I know nothing against
myself**; I am free from the blood of all men; I have kept back
nothing profitable to you. However, I am not vindicated by
my own opinion; it is the Lord himself who examines and
judges me as a servant and minister.'

v.5. 'Therefore, be slow in your judgement and be not hasty
to pass sentence nor to censure one another, particularly your
ministers.' There is a time fixed for the judgement of all things,
that is, the day of our Lord's return. When he comes, he will
bring to light the secret things that are now hidden in darkness
and will disclose the aims, motives and purposes of hearts.
Then every regenerate soul, every true believer and every
faithful minister will hear God say, 'Well done, good and
faithful servant.' However much a true minister is despised and
criticized now, in that day he will be exalted.

v.6. 'I have applied all this discussion about factions and
divisions to myself and Apollos (1 Cor. 3:4-7) for your sakes,
so that, from what I have said of us, as illustrations, you may
learn to think of ministers and all men according to the
Scriptures (Rom. 12:3). Learn to appreciate men's gifts and
usefulness; yet do not ascribe too much to them lest some be
puffed up, inflated with pride and begin to set one against
another.

v.7. This question and that which follows are addressed to
the members of this church who were glorying in and setting
one minister against another. 'Who distinguished you? Who
called you out of darkness into his grace? Who gave you the
gift to minister, to hear, or to believe? Therefore, you ought
not to glory in yourselves nor in your ministers, but in God!'
He is the fountain of all grace and knowledge. To glory in any
mercy, favour, or blessing, as if it were owing to human
wisdom or power, betrays wretched pride and ignorance
(John 3:27; James 1:17).

v.8. 'In your opinion you are full, you have arrived, you feel
no need of growth, instruction and correction. Like the
Laodiceans you say, "We are rich and have need of nothing."
You think yourselves rich in spiritual gifts and graces. You
think you reign as kings, without any need for counsel or
instructions from the apostles and ministers. You have ascended
your throne and come into your kingdom. I wish the reigning

time for the church had come, then we would all reign with
Christ and you! But alas, it is evident from your behaviour
that you are neither full, rich, nor do you reign, but rather you
have need of much teaching and correction. You are but
children in understanding, needing milk instead of meat. You
are far from being what you think yourselves to be' (1 Cor.
3:1-3).

Be ye followers of me

1 Corinthians 4 : 9-21

These Corinthians were lifted up with pride. In their opinion
they had arrived and needed no instructions, correction, nor
guidance from Paul and the other apostles. They thought
themselves rich in gifts, knowledge and grace. It was evident
from their behaviour that they were neither full nor rich, but
were children in understanding, far from being what they
thought themselves to be (Rom. 12:3).

v.9. **'It seems to be that God has made an exhibit of us
apostles.'** He may refer to the great triumphal processions
when conquering armies marched through the city. Their
slaves and enemies, sentenced to death, were at the end of the
line, taunted, persecuted and jeered by all spectators. **'We are
made a sport and spectacle to wicked men and before the
angels.'**

v.10. **'We are** looked upon as **fools** for our devotion to and
our preaching of Christ crucified, but you, supposedly, have
made such use of worldly wisdom and carnal policy in your
religion that you have gained the favour of the world and
escaped persecution. **We are weak** in body, influence, worldly
goods and fame, **but you are strong!** You have property,
earthly credentials, friends in high places and much influence

and acclaim. **You are honoured** among men for your learning,
your riches and your success, **but we are** held in contempt and
despised of men.'

vv.11-13.   In an effort to curb their pride and to warn them
against the friendship of this world, Paul continues to describe
the real attitude toward and the treatment of a devoted
witness of Christ by this world (Isa. 53:3; Luke 6:22-26;
John 15:18, 19). 'We have gone both hungry and thirsty; we
have few clothes; we are scourged and beaten and wander
about having no place to call home. We have to work with our
hands to make a living. When men revile, curse and ridicule us,
we bless them. When we are persecuted for Christ's sake, we
take it patiently. When we are slandered, we try to answer
softly. We are considered to be the rubbish and the filth of this
world — the scum of the earth.'

v.14.   Paul did not write these things to put the Corinthians
to shame, though they certainly should have been ashamed of
the vain opinion they had of themselves. He wrote to warn
them of the dangers of compromise, worldly wisdom, being
lifted up with pride and discounting the ministry of the
apostles (Gal. 3:1-3,9-11).

v.15.   'Though you have many preachers and teachers (some
false and some true), yet you only have one spiritual father,
who was the instrument of God to bring you to a knowledge
of Christ. It was under my ministry that you were regenerated
and brought to faith. It was not the ministry of law and works
but the gospel of Christ which was the means of your salvation'
(Rom. 3:19-26).

v.16.   'So I urge and implore you not to depart from my
teaching but to abide in the doctrine of Christ. Do not follow
those who would draw you away and cause divisions among
you. Follow me as I follow Christ' (Heb. 13:7).

v.17.   'Because I care for you and your spiritual welfare and

growth, I sent Timothy unto you. Timothy is like a son to me
and is a faithful steward of grace and the gospel of Christ.
Timothy will bring to your remembrance my way of preaching,
the doctrines I taught and what should be the manner of life
and conversation of believers. He will remind you that the sum
and substance of faith, life and hope is Christ. This I teach and
preach everywhere in all churches.'

v.18. 'Some are conceited, arrogant and puffed up over their
gifts, their stations in the church and their human wisdom,
hoping that I will not come back and call them to account for
their errors.'

v.19. 'But I will come if the Lord is willing, and I will
perceive and understand the truth about these proud boasters.
I will not observe the outward show, the fine words and the
claims to fame, but I will expose the truth about them that
their power is not to the glory of God, the good of the church
and the conversion of sinners' (2 Tim. 3:5).

v.20. The kingdom of God consists not of fine talk, human
words and wisdom, philosophy and vain show, but in the
powerful efficacy of the Spirit attending the preaching of the
gospel. God awakens, convicts, converts and brings men to
Christ, making them new creatures inwardly (1 Cor. 2:1-5).

v.21. 'Now which do you prefer? Shall I come to you with a
rod of correction, as an apostle of Christ, to set things straight
in the church? Or shall I come to you with the affection of a
father, with a pleasant countenance and a meek spirit, rejoicing
over your determination to set matters straight?'

Church discipline exercised

1 Corinthians 5 : 1-13

Having rebuked the Corinthians for the divisions and factions among them, the apostle gives another reason why they had no right to be proud and arrogant. They allowed members of the congregation to live in sin and open transgressions without condemning or disciplining them.

v.1. 'It is common knowledge in and around Corinth that there is sexual immorality among you. The church cannot plead ignorance in the matter, for it is known by all.' This particular incident was a man living in open incest with his father's wife. Almost all writers agree that it was his stepmother, for there is a distinction between a mother and a father's wife (Deut. 22:30; 27:20-23). Such conduct was not even permitted among pagan Gentiles.

v.2. Equally shocking to the apostle was the fact that the church was not grieved by this man's actions but rather held him in esteem and overlooked his way of life. He may have been a teacher, preacher, or gifted man, and the church applauded him, rather than praying that he be removed from their midst.

vv.3-5. Paul declared that though he was absent from them in body, yet certainly with them in spirit, he had already decided what should be done about this situation.

When the church is met together in the Spirit of Christ, with the power and authority of Christ, this man is to be delivered into the hands of Satan for the destruction of his body that his soul may yet be saved in the day of our Lord Jesus (1 Tim. 1:20). Let us exercise care here because this is

apostolic authority and power, not to be played with by just
anyone. Paul said in verse 3, **'I have judged** this case.' And in
verse 4 he said, **'When you are gathered together, and my
spirit, with the authority of Christ'.** The **'destruction of his
flesh'** is the shaking, afflicting and buffeting of his flesh that
he might be brought to repentance and restoration.

v.6.   They gloried in their prosperity, in their riches and
wealth, in their ministers and in their wisdom and gifts. Even
in the midst of such immorality, they gloried! This is not
good! You know that a little leaven, permitted, let alone and
uncorrected, will affect the whole body. Whether this be false
doctrine, a carnal spirit, immorality or ungodliness, if a stop is
not put to it, it increases to more evil and ungodliness. We are
to be compassionate, understanding and forgiving, but known
sin is to be judged, condemned and put away.

v.7.   'Purge out the incestuous person as the Jews of old
purged their houses of leaven just before the Passover' (Exod.
23:18; 34:25). (Leaven is a small piece of fermenting dough
and is typical of corruption and decay. It was forbidden in all
sacrifices.) 'Rid yourselves of this open evil that you may
appear to be what you profess to be — new creatures in Christ,
walking in newness of life, keeping the true and spiritual
passover, for Christ, our Passover, has been sacrificed for us.'

v.8.   'Therefore, let us keep the Lord's Table, worship our
Lord, fellowship in the blessings and benefits of his grace and
preach his gospel, not in the old, sinful, worldly manner of
life as before conversion (with malice, division, strife and
immorality), but in godliness, holiness, sincerity and truth
(2 Cor. 5:17).

vv.9-11.   'I wrote you in another epistle not to associate
closely and habitually with wicked men who openly compromise the principles of righteousness.' Evidently the apostle
wrote other epistles that are not included in the Scriptures.
'I do not mean that you are to have no dealings commercially

or in conversation with fornicators and evil men who make no profession of religion. In order to obey such a command, you would have to get out of the world altogether. But if a man professes to know Christ, is a member of the body of Christ and is known to be guilty of immorality, greed, idolatry, has a foul tongue, is a drunkard or a thief and remains impenitent, you are to separate him from your company.'

vv.12, 13.   'It is neither my business nor yours to judge people outside the church. We have no power over them. God is their judge. But it is the business of the church not only to exhort, encourage and edify one another, but to rebuke, reprove and correct the things that are contrary to the Word of God. Therefore, this man who lives in incest is to be put out of the church.'

Brother against brother before unbelievers

1 Corinthians 6 : 1-8

In these eight verses the apostle exposes another fault in the Corinthian church — taking one another to court before unbelievers to settle their differences. The rebuke consists of two parts:

1. Our differences ought to be settled among ourselves on the basis of love and grace, not before the wicked, who know nothing of either. Not to be able to do this makes the gospel we believe to be held in contempt by wicked men.

2. True believers ought to endure injuries and misunderstandings with patience, love and forgiveness, rather than seeking revenge and compensation.

v.1.   Paul expressed surprise that one believer, with a complaint against another believer, would dare to take the matter to a court of law to be decided by unbelievers. He is not condemning courts of law or magistrates (who must administer justice to all) nor those who are summoned to court and must appear to maintain their cause. He is rather condemning those who bring their brethren into such situations when it is in their power to employ other remedies.

v. 2.   When we seek the judgement and advice of unbelieving lawyers and magistrates, we are insinuating that there is no one in the society of the godly who is qualified to settle our disputes. True believers are endowed with spiritual wisdom and will one day judge the world, for they shall reign with Christ! Are they then not capable or worthy to deal with minor, personal matters? Noah, by his faith and obedience, in a sense judged and condemned the world (Heb. 11:7). The judges of this world are not qualified to judge spiritual matters. The basis of their judgement is 'an eye for an eye', while the foundation of our judgement is mercy and grace (1 Cor. 2:14, 15).

v. 3.   Even the angels are subject to the Word of God which we preach (Gal. 1:8). But the reference here is probably to the fallen angels who are already under judgement (Jude 6). When we believe the Word, bow to the will of God and look to Christ for redemption (while they do not), it is clear that we act in wisdom and righteousness (and they act foolishly). This is to judge them and their action. If, by the grace of God, a believer can discern heavenly things, can he not much more deal with the things which pertain to the earth?

v. 4.   The Authorized Version is not as clear on this verse as some others. All agree that Paul continues his rebuke and is saying, 'When you have cases of everyday life to decide, why do you set these matters before such men as lawyers, judges and outsiders, who have no standing in the church, have no esteem and are of no account to the church?'

v. 5.   **'I say this to move you to shame.** You certainly ought to be ashamed of yourselves. Can it be that there is not in your fellowship one wise man who is competent enough to decide grievances, disputes and quarrels between brothers? You boast of your wisdom and gifts, yet you deny it all by your actions.'

v. 6.   The brother relationship here is spiritual, for we are all sons of God, born again and one family in Christ. **'Brother goes to court against brother, and that before unbelievers.'** This is a serious and shameful thing, for it brings reproach on the name of Christ and on the church.

vv. 7, 8.   'This is not only shameful, but it indicates a serious defect in you. It admits to defeat and is another evidence of carnality (1 Cor. 3:3). Instead of seeking revenge or legal settlement, why not rather take the wrong? Why not let the brother have his way? Rather than go to court, cause division or upset the fellowship, bear injustices patiently and thereby glorify Christ' (Luke 6:27-36). It is more advisable for a believer to suffer wrong, and even to be cheated, than for him to go to court with his brother.

Instead of this, it is you who do wrong and defraud your own brethren by treating them in this manner.

Ye are not your own

1 Corinthians 6 : 9-20

In the preceding chapters and verses Paul dealt with a matter of incest — open sin in the assembly. Then he warned them about keeping company with those who profess Christ, yet are fornicators, covetous, idolators, drunkards and extortioners. In this chapter he expresses shock over the fact that some of them were taking fellow-believers to court before unbelievers. In the verses before us he contends that such behaviour, if not repented of, shows that such persons are destitute of the grace of God and unfit for the kingdom of God, regardless of their profession!

vv. 9, 10. Without the righteousness of Christ, there will be
no entrance into the presence and kingdom of God (Matt.
5:20; Heb. 12:14). Christ is our righteousness and sanctification
(2 Cor. 5:21; 1 Cor. 1:30). But he is also speaking of an
imparted righteousness and a new life which every believer has
experienced in Christ (2 Cor. 5:17; Rom. 6:12-15). Do not
be deceived nor imagine that you shall be saved while you
continue to live in sin and wickedness. Those who practise
these evil deeds shall not inherit the kingdom of God.

v. 11. 'Some of you who are now children of God, saved by
his free grace, were guilty of these very sins, but **you have been
washed**, cleansed and forgiven in and by the blood of Christ.
You have been sanctified.' He is not speaking here of the fact
that they were set apart by the Father in divine election
(though they were), or of the fact that in Christ they have a
perfect righteousness and sanctification imputed to them
(though they did); but the sanctification of the Holy Spirit
(which lies in a principle of new life, new nature, new heart
and new desires) has been created in the believer. He does not
just *claim* to be a new person; he *is* a new person. He loves
holiness and hates sin! (Rom. 7:22-25.) '**You are** also **justified**
before God. All sin is put away and you are accepted in the
Beloved, not by works, but you also delight to do his will and
glorify his name.'

v. 12. '**All things are permissible for me**' (certainly no fornication, idolatry, drunkenness, adultery, or such), that is, the
things which are not explicitly forbidden in the Word of God
(such as foods, drinks and material pleasures). 'But all these
things are not necessarily helpful to me nor good for me. When
these indifferent things destroy my fellowship, peace and
comfort, or cause a weak brother to stumble, they become
wrong. Therefore, I will not become a slave to my appetite,
desires or fleshly wants. I regard even the indifferent things of
the world in the light of my relationship with Christ and his

church and can set them aside for his glory.'

vv. 13, 14.   Though food is intended for the body and the body for food, yet this cannot be said of sexual immorality, which some of the Corinthians and the Gentiles took to be as indifferent as food and drink. We must satisfy the craving of the body for food and drink, whatever food is available, but sexual desires are to be met in a state of marriage, not promiscuously (1 Cor. 7:2). Our bodies are intended to serve and glorify him in righteousness and holiness and at the last to be raised by him and made like to his glorious body (Phil. 3:20, 21).

vv. 15-17.   We were chosen in Christ, given to him and made one with him, our bodies as well as our souls. We are redeemed by him and in union with him. **'Shall I take the members of Christ and make them members of a prostitute?'** This would be an absurd and sinful thing. One who engages in union with a prostitute becomes one with her, even as the Lord spoke of husband and wife (legally and spiritually) becoming one flesh. But he who is united with Christ by grace and faith is one spirit with him. This union is a spiritual one, complete and perfect.

v. 18.   'Shun immorality and all sexual looseness; flee from impurity in word, thought or deed.' Most sins that a man commits are committed by the abuse of other things and do not bring hurt and reproach on the body as sexual immorality does. The body is defiled, dishonoured and disgraced by immoral conduct.

v. 19.   What is said in 1 Corinthians 3:16, 17 of saints in general is said here of our bodies in particular. The Spirit of God dwells in us, and we are not our own; we belong to him. We are not our own masters to live to satisfy our lusts, nor to abuse these temples. We are his by creation, by choice and by covenant.

v.20. We were redeemed by Christ; therefore, we are to glorify him in all things! (Col. 3:17.)

Building a happy marriage

1 Corinthians 7 : 1-11

Some of the Corinthians had written to Paul asking his advice and counsel on matters pertaining to marriage. In these verses Paul talks about the advantages, nature, duties and permanence of marriage.

v.1. It is not unlawful to marry, nor sinful to lie with a woman in wedlock (Gen. 2:18-25; 1:27, 28; Heb. 13:4). Paul is simply saying that if a person has the gift of self-restraint and no need for sexual expression, he would be better off unmarried. While a good marriage produces happiness, fulfilment and companionship, it carries with it heavy responsibilities, personal sacrifice and certain troubles and sorrows in the flesh (v.28).

v.2. 'To avoid sexual immorality and unlawful relationships, let every man have a wife to love and enjoy and let every woman have a husband to share her life and meet her needs.'

v.3. 'Let the husband render unto the wife all the offices of love — tenderness, kindness, provisions, protection and respect.' But the chief reference here is to the marriage bed and her sexual needs. Likewise, the wife is to be aware of the needs of her husband and to meet those needs willingly; otherwise, she is called by the ancient writers 'a rebellious wife'. According to the Song of Solomon, this relationship, when properly understood (free from traditional guilt and false piety, and knowing it is ordained of God with his blessings), ceases to be a duty and becomes joy and pleasure.

v.4. A wife does not have exclusive authority over and ownership of her body to refrain the use of it from her husband, to give it to someone else, to neglect it, nor to abuse it. The husband has a power over and right to her body. The same is true of the husband's body, to which the wife has certain rights. Better to recognize this as a joy rather than a duty or an unpleasant task. Happy are the wife and husband who find delight in pleasing each other with an attractive, clean and loving person and personality.

v.5. 'Fraud' is a strong word, but to refuse love and affection where it is needed and to deprive each other of that which it is in our power to give is selfish and evil. A lazy husband who will not work and support his family fails as a husband; likewise, a wife who fails in her marriage responsibilities to her husband is a fraud. 'You may interrupt marital relationship in time of special spiritual burdens, trials and fastings, but only by mutual consent and only briefly, lest one of you be tempted to find satisfaction elsewhere.'

v.6. What Paul says in verse 5 about parting for a time and coming together again is not a command of God, but he speaks it by permission. This time of separation (for whatever reason) is neither essential nor required, but only according to their own wishes.

v.7. Paul speaks here of the gift of self-control and abstinence, which he covets for all believers that we might not be in danger of temptation and that our minds and thoughts might be more on Christ, not the flesh. It would be a blessing to be rid of all fleshly thoughts and desires, yet each has his own special gift from God, one of this kind and one of another.

v.8. If a man or woman is unmarried and chooses to remain that way (not that it is sinful to marry again), it would be better for them; for they would be more free from the cares of this life, have less trouble and be free to serve Christ. Paul was unmarried, had no home nor children, and was free to devote his entire time to the gospel (vv.32, 33).

v.9. If a person does not have the gift of self-control in this area, he should seek a wife, and the woman a husband. It is much better to marry than to be aflame with passion and tortured by desire.

v.10. As indicated, some of the above was spoken by permission and given as good advice; but this is a commandment! What he is about to say, we are under obligation to observe, because this is a law of God! 'A wife is not to leave her husband!' (Matt. 19:6; Gen. 2:24.) Marriage vows are not to be taken lightly. Neither husband nor wife is at liberty to separate from the other because of disagreement, disease, or even differences in matters of faith.

v.11. If a person cannot be prevailed upon to remain with his or her partner but leaves for some reason, that person is to remain unmarried; his departure does not make the marriage void. 'Remain unmarried or be reconciled to your husband or wife.'

Continue in the station wherein you were called

1 Corinthians 7 : 12-24

In the preceding verse the apostle gave a strong and direct commandment to married believers: **'Let not the wife depart from her husband and let not the husband put away his wife.'** There is no debate nor argument to be heard.

vv.12, 13. To the believer who is married to an unbeliever, Paul offers his counsel and advice. He is saying that he has no commandment from the Lord in regard to this matter, but if a believer is married to an unbeliever and that unbeliever consents to live in harmony and peace with the believer, do not depart.

v.14. The unbelieving husband or wife is espoused or legally married in the eyes of God to the believer. They are rightly and legally husband and wife regardless of their differences concerning the gospel. If a person is converted to Christ and his partner is not, this does not dissolve the marriage nor make it unholy in God's sight. If their marriage were not legal and holy, children born to them would be illegitimate. But children born to this type of marriage are, in a legal and civil sense, as holy as children born to believing parents.

v.15. If the unbeliever should leave the believer on account of the gospel (in hatred of it) and will not live with the believer unless Christ is denied or truth compromised, let him leave. The deserted person may live in peace, being not to blame; for a brother or sister is bound in conscience to obey in things pertaining to worship and the service and glory of Christ. Nor is the believer bound to remain unmarried in such cases but is free to marry another, only in the Lord. Desertion in such cases (for the sake of the gospel) is a breach of the marriage contract; otherwise, a brother or sister would be in subjection and bondage to the rebel for the rest of his or her life. God has called us to a peaceful life in the church and in the home.

v.16. If a believer is married to an unbeliever and they can build a life of peace together, it may be that the unbeliever will, by the witness and behaviour of the believer, be brought' to a saving interest in Christ. 'Continue to live together, if possible, for the glory of Christ and the eternal welfare of all concerned.'

v.17. This word is placed here with regard to all that is said before and all that follows. It has respect to every man's proper gift and station in life, whether as a single person or married, whether married to a believer or an unbeliever, and to the examples which follow. God has distributed our gifts as to nature and grace. He has given us the place we are to fill, the business we must follow and the area of usefulness in his kingdom. So when he calls us and reveals his grace to us, wherever we are and whatever we are, let us be content with his good providence and walk with him.

vv.18, 19. If a man is a Jew, being circumcised in infancy, and has embraced the Lord Jesus, there is no reason for him to be uneasy or take methods to remove this mark from his flesh because it has been fulfilled and abolished by Christ. If a man is a Gentile, has never been circumcised and is called by grace, let him not submit to circumcision for religious purposes. In the affair of justification before God, circumcision is nothing! It cannot make a man righteous or unrighteous before God. The commandments of our Lord and Saviour are to be observed from the principle of love and with a view to the glory of God.

v.20. Coming to know Christ does not require that a man change his business, his marriage, or his station in life as a servant or master, unless that station in life is unlawful according to the Word, or dishonest, or detrimental to his Christian life and testimony (2 Kings 5:18, 19).

v.21. 'Were you a slave or a servant when you were called to Christ? Do not be troubled by it or be anxious to be otherwise. Be a good servant, serve your master faithfully, and do not look upon a lowly position or hard work as a contradiction of your call. If you are able to gain your freedom and better your position, avail yourself of the opportunity.'

v.22. The reason a believer should be content to be a slave, a servant, or whatever, is because he that is called by grace, though a servant in a civil sense, is the Lord's freeman in a spiritual sense, and he that is free in a civil sense when called is the bond-servant of Christ (Rom. 1:1).

vv.23, 24. We are bought with the price of Christ's blood and, whether servants or masters, we are the servants of Christ,

not of men. So in whatever station, state or condition of life
we were when called, let us continue there until it please God
in his providence to change it.

More about marriage

1 Corinthians 7 : 25-40

v. 25.   In these verses the apostle returns to the subject of
marriage and addresses first those who have never been married.
What he is about to say to them is not by a law or commandment of God, but is his own opinion and advice, with sincerity,
as one counted faithful by the Lord himself.

v. 26.   'My opinion,' declares the apostle, 'is that, because of
this time of persecution, affliction and distress, it would be
better if believers remained unmarried.' Believers were put in
prison, driven from place to place and life in general was most
difficult.

v. 27.   He advises those who are married by no means to
desert one another nor seek to dissolve the marriage bond;
on the other hand, if they are free from a wife, it would be
better not to seek one.

v. 28.   If a person who has never been married, or one who
has been legally freed from a wife, think it fit to be married,
he commits no sin. It is not a sin to be married. But those who
choose married life shall have physical and earthly troubles,
and Paul is concerned that they be spared from these troubles.

v. 29.   Our days on earth are so short and full of trouble that
an unmarried state is preferable. As for those who are married,
it would be wise for them to give themselves to the worship of
God, his gospel and his glory, both publicly and privately, and

not be taken up overmuch with family and personal cares.

vv.30, 31.   Every worldly relationship, sorrow, joy, possession
and care is fading and perishing (Job. 1:21). Nothing about
this world is permanent nor lasting. We may weep, but weeping
endures for the night; joy comes in the morning. We may
rejoice in earthly treasure, but only temporarily. We may buy
and sell, but we really own nothing. Let us use the world and
its material and physical qualities with a loose hand, neither
too much depressed by its sadness nor too much elated over its
joys. It will all pass away.

v.32.   The apostle's earnest desire is to have believers as free
as possible from entangling physical, emotional and material
cares that accompany marriage. The unmarried man is more at
leisure and can more conveniently care for the things that have
to do with grace and glory.

vv.33, 34.   The married man must attend to business, provide
food and clothing, educate and discipline children and make
his family comfortable. He must be involved to a greater
extent in the world than the unmarried man. The same is true
of women, as stated in verse 34.

v.35.   Paul said these things to them for their own welfare
and profit, not to put restrictions and burdens on them which
they could not bear, but to promote their comfort and good,
that they might attend to the things of God without distraction
from worldly cares.

v.36.   If a man's daughter reaches the age for marriage and
desires to be married, he should not take this opinion of the
apostle and force her to remain unmarried. The father should
give his blessing to the marriage. No one sins in this regard,
neither the father nor the couple.

v.37.   But where there is no necessity for marriage, where the
woman or man has the gift of continency and is determined

not to be married, there is no shame nor reproach in remaining single any more than in being married.

v.38.   The parents who give their daughters and sons in marriage do well. The parents who are not pressured by tradition or custom and allow their children to remain unmarried with parental help and blessings, do better.

v.39.   While a husband is living, the believing wife is bound by God's law to continue to live with him, but when he is dead, she is free to marry whom she will, providing that he, too, is a believer! No true believer is free to marry an unbeliever and expect God's blessing.

v.40.   In the apostle's opinion, a widow will be happier if she remains unmarried. He adds, 'I think I have the mind of the Spirit in this matter.'

Christian liberty with love and wisdom

1 Corinthians 8 : 1-13

In this chapter the apostle deals with the subject of eating meat which has been used in sacrifices to idols. Pagans offered sacrifices of sheep, oxen and other cattle to their idol gods and then used the meat for food at feasts in their temples, in their homes, or else sold it in the markets. The question arose among the Corinthians whether it was lawful for believers to eat this meat. Evidently some were buying the meat for use at home and some were even going to the feasts in the temple of idols and eating the meat there. This question was also considered in the council of Jerusalem (Acts 15:28,29).

v.1.   'Now about meat offered to idols: of course, we all know that an idol is nothing but a block of wood or stone and

cannot defile a believer, but some of us do not think it fit to
make use of this knowledge of Christian liberty to the wound-
ing and grieving of other believers.' Some of the weaker
brethren were convinced that it was wrong to eat this meat
and were offended when they saw it done. The reply they
received was 'We know an idol is nothing!' Paul says, 'We all
know that, but knowledge without wisdom, love and consideration for others leads to pride, conceit and division.' **'Love
edifies,'** that is, a man who has knowledge joined with love for
God and others will seek that which is edifying and profitable
to others. Without this attitude and spirit, his knowledge is
worthless.

v.2.   This is true in any matter. If anyone imagines that he
has come to know and understand much of divine things and
does not use that knowledge with wisdom, love for others and
regard for the glory of God and the peace of the church, he
knows nothing yet as he ought to know. If he did, he would
know that even the Lord pleased not himself (Rom. 15:1-3).

v.3.   If a man truly loves God, he will show that love for God
by loving his brother (being careful not to hinder or offend
him), making use of his knowledge and liberty for the edification of others (1 John 4:20). That man will be approved of
God, blessed by God and used for God's glory.

vv.4-6.   'We know that a pagan idol is nothing'; it has no real
existence, no meaning, no power, no value. 'We know that
there is no god but the living God' (Deut. 6:4, 5). There are
many so-called gods of pagan men, whether in heaven (sun,
moon, stars, angels, dead men and women who are venerated)
or earth (creatures, statues, or whatever). Yet for us there is
only one God, the Father, who is the fountain and source of
all things (Acts 17:28). There is one Redeemer, the Lord
Jesus Christ, by whom God created all things (John 1:3;
Col. 1:16-18), by whom God redeemed the elect, and by
whom he reconciled the world to himself.

v. 7. 'But there are some Christians (former idolaters) who were all their lives accustomed to thinking of a certain idol as real and living, who, if they saw you eat this meat, would be offended, and if they ate of it, their weak consciences would be injured.'

v. 8. What the Christian liberty advocates asserted is positively true. The type of food we eat will not cause our acceptance by God nor will it separate us from God. Whether we eat this meat or leave it has nothing to do with our relationship to God in Christ (Rom. 14:17).

v. 9. But we are to be careful that our personal liberty and understanding do not become a hindrance or a cause of stumbling to a weak brother. This would be a violation of brotherly love (Rom. 14:13-15; Gal. 5:13, 14).

vv. 10, 11. 'Suppose a weak brother (who does not have a clear understanding of Christian liberty) should see you (who are learned, mature and knowledgeable) sitting eating in an idol's temple. He may be led by your example to do the same thing against his conscience, knowledge and understanding. In doing so, he violates his principles, which may lead to other careless and more serious infractions and the ultimate ruin of a dear brother for whom Christ died.

v. 12. 'When you, by example, draw men into practices contrary to their consciences and principles, you sin against Christ.' Knowing that the brother is offended and that eating this meat is against his judgement, leading him to do so is not love for Christ or the brother; therefore, it is sin.

v. 13. 'Therefore, if my eating a certain food is the cause of my brother's falling or hinders his spiritual growth, I will not eat this meat lest I cause him to stumble.'

Supporting the ministry

1 Corinthians 9 : 1-14

In the greater part of this chapter Paul continues speaking on the subject of Christian liberty and its proper use. It is our duty to deny ourselves of even that which is lawful if it is genuinely offensive to our brother. He uses himself as an example, having denied himself in three things: eating and drinking at their expense, marriage and requiring financial support for his labour among them. All were lawful to him, but he denied himself for their sakes who were weak in the faith.

vv. 1, 2.   Some denied that Paul was an apostle because he was not one of the original twelve. He refutes the charge saying, **'I am free.'** No man had authority over him. He was chosen, ordained, taught and sent forth as an apostle by Christ (Gal. 1:11, 12, 15-18). **'I have seen the Lord.'** All apostles were eye-witnesses of his glory (Acts 10:39-42; 1 John 1:1, 2). Paul saw Christ on the Damascus Road and when he was taken to the third heaven. 'But,' he adds, 'if others deny my apostleship, surely you Corinthians will not; for the effects of my ministry among you puts you past denial. You are living proof of God's hand on me.'

v. 3.   This is his ground of defence, the vindication of his apostleship and himself to those who would criticize and question him: 'I have authority directly from Christ. I am an eye-witness of his glory. The fruits of my ministry are proof of my apostleship!'

vv. 4, 5.   Having proved his apostleship, Paul proceeds to establish his right to support and maintenance as a gospel minister. 'Do I not have the right to food and drink at the expense of those to whom I minister? Do I not have a right to take along with me a wife, as do the other apostles — James, John, Peter and those who were near kinsmen to our Lord?'

v. 6. 'Or is it only Barnabas and I who have no right to refrain from manual labour for a livelihood, in order to give our full time to the gospel ministry?' Paul worked with his hands in his trade at Corinth (Acts 18:1-3; 20:33, 34; 1 Thess. 2:9). While at many places he did not exercise his right of support, he nevertheless defended it.

v. 7. By three examples commonly known among men, Paul shows it to be reasonable that ministers of the gospel should be supported by the people to whom they minister.

1. What soldier serves in an army and goes to war for a nation at his own expense?

2. What man plants a vineyard and does not eat some of the fruit?

3. Who tends a flock and does not drink the milk and eat the meat?

v. 8. 'Do I say this as a man reasons and only on human authority? Does not the Word of God teach the same also?'

v. 9. 'It is written in Deuteronomy 25:4: 'You shall not put a muzzle on an ox when he treads out the corn, in order to keep him from eating of it.' God looked upon this as an act of cruelty. Does God care more for oxen than he does for his ministers?

v. 10. It is true that Deuteronomy 25:4 mentions oxen in particular; but it is a principle that is to be applied to all our dealings with those who labour and serve us, especially those who minister the all-important Word of God. He who ploughs for another ought to work with the hope of getting bread for himself, and he who works in the threshing-floor ought to labour in the hope of being cared for by those for whom he labours (1 Tim. 5:17, 18).

v. 11. 'If we have studied, preached and taught you the doctrines of the Word of God and you have profited spiritually through our constant labour, is it asking too much if we share in your material possessions, such as food, drink and clothing?'

v. 12. 'Other preachers among you justly claim and enjoy your support. Do not Barnabas and I have an even greater claim, being the first ministers to preach the gospel to you, and I, being an apostle of Christ? Yet I did not exercise this privilege of support while I was labouring among you, lest someone charge me with covetousness and hinder the spread of the gospel.'

v. 13. 'You can understand the mind and will of God under the New Testament by studying the mind and will of God under the Old Testament. God has a ministry under the Old Testament (the tribe of Levi), and he appointed a livelihood for them' (Num. 18:20, 21; Deut. 18:1).

v. 14. God's will for his ministers is the same under the New Testament. It is his will that those who have set aside worldly employment to spend their time in the study and preaching of the gospel should have a livelihood from their labour.

Total dedication to his gospel

1 Corinthians 9 : 15-27

In the preceding verses the apostle clearly shows from the Scriptures that the Lord's apostles, ministers, evangelists and missionaries (who are engaged full time in the study and preaching of the gospel) should be supported and cared for by those to whom they minister.

v.15. 'Though I have the right to marry as well as others, to forego secular labour and to expect maintenance by those to whom I preach, yet I have not made use of these privileges; nor am I now writing and suggesting that these things be done for me.' Evidently Paul had been accused of preaching for gain and for his own profit and advantage. He continually rejected and denied the charge! That is why he chose to work with his hands, providing his own upkeep and taking nothing from the Corinthians (Acts 20:33, 34; 2 Cor. 11:7-10; 12:17, 18). Paul gloried and rejoiced in the fact that no one could accuse him of using the ministry to get gain, and now he had rather die than be deprived of this personal satisfaction.

v.16. 'Though I do preach the gospel of God's glory and grace, I have no room nor reason to glory, nor even to feel that I have done anything unusual or commendable; for I am a servant of God, under divine orders, and exposed to severe penalty and woe if I do not preach the gospel.'

v.17. 'If I preach this gospel and endure the trials and labour in the Word with a willing spirit and a cheerful heart, I have great satisfaction and compensation; but if I do so reluctantly and under compulsion, I am still a servant of Christ, entrusted with a sacred and holy commission, whether with pay or without pay, whether willingly or reluctantly. None of these things changes the fact that I am a servant of Christ with divine orders to preach the Word.'

v.18. 'What then is my present compensation and reward? Just this: that I am so in love with Christ, so convinced of the truth of his gospel, so burdened for all men, that I surrender my rights and privileges as a preacher of the gospel and give my services free to all. I cannot be accused of profiting from the gospel or abusing my privileges.'

v.19. Paul declared that he was free from all (the word 'men' is not in the original text), from the curse of the moral law, from the yoke of the ceremonial law and from the maintenance and support of believers. Yet he considered himself the willing servant of all, catering to them in every way that he could in order to endear himself to them and bring them to faith in Christ.

vv. 20-22. The ceremonial law died with Christ (Eph. 2:15, 16). Believers are not bound by circumcision, sabbaths and other rituals prescribed under the law, but Paul observed some of these in order to have an open door to preach to the Jews (Acts 16:1-3; 21:19-24). To the Gentiles, who were under no obligation to the ceremonial law, Paul could freely discouse and fellowship as one under the law of Christ. With the weak (those without discernment and maturity), who were troubled about meats, drinks and various forms of liberty, he identified, surrendered his liberty and played down his knowledge, that he might gain their confidence. In short, he became all things to all men that he might, at any cost to himself and in any way, bring them to a saving knowledge of Christ.

v. 23. Paul had two great ends at which he aimed in this denial of himself in these many points of liberty: chiefly, for the gospel's sake, that is, for the glory of God, for the spread of the gospel to the eternal glory of our Redeemer; secondly, that Jew and Gentile (men of all sorts) might share with him in the blessings of eternal life (2 Tim. 2:9, 10).

v. 24. The reference in this and the following verses is to the Grecian games, such as running, wrestling and fighting. Many start the race, many run for a while, but the one who obtains the prize is the one who finishes the race first. The object of running is to gain the crown given to the victor. Believers are to run the Christian race, persevering with one object in view, and that is to reign with Christ and be made like him (Ps. 17:15). Nothing is to divert their attention or interest from this goal.

v. 25. Every athlete who competes in the games is mindful of the need to discipline himself in food, drink, pleasures and idleness. He restricts himself to temperance and moderation in all things in order to win a temporary and corruptible crown. The believer's faith, dedication, temperance and sacrifice are for a higher and nobler purpose — to gain an incorruptible crown! (Heb. 12:1, 2.)

vv. 26, 27. 'Therefore, I do not run as one who is out jogging with no goal or destination, but as one who strives to cross the finish line. I do not box as a man shadow-boxes, who has no opponent, but only strikes out at the air. I have a real enemy — the flesh! So I discipline my flesh, my mind, my body and bring them into subjection to the Spirit of Christ. I subdue this flesh with its desires and infirmities, lest while preaching the gospel to others, I myself should fail the test and prove to be reprobate' (2 Cor. 13:5).

Warnings from the wilderness

1 Corinthians 10 : 1-13

Many in the church at Corinth were puffed up with their knowledge, their gifts and the great privileges with which God had blessed them. They had a good foundation laid by Paul (1 Cor. 3:10, 11), they knew the gospel (1 Cor. 15:1-4) and theirs was a mighty church, respected and well known by all. But factions, divisions, open sin, intellectualism, and all sorts of ideas and wrong practices had crept into their midst. Therefore, to warn them of vain presumption, false confidence and indifference to holy conduct and practice, Paul sets before them the example of Israel, the church in the wilderness. All of these Israelites enjoyed great God-given privileges, the special favour of God and were exposed to the gospel of Christ in type, yet most of them perished under God's judgement in the wilderness.

v.1. 'I would not have you to be ignorant nor uninformed concerning the matter of perseverance in faith, in obedience and in conduct becoming a believer. All of the people of Israel were led by the cloud (in which God's presence went before them), and every one of them passed safely through the Red Sea.'

v.2. 'Every one of them allowed himself to be baptized unto Moses in the cloud and in the sea,' which was an acknowledgement of their regard unto him as their guide and governor, which is a picture of our baptism, which identifies us with Christ.

v.3. Those who perished in the wilderness all ate the same spiritual (supernaturally given) food which Moses, Caleb and Joshua ate (who went into Canaan). Manna is called spiritual food, firstly, because it was bread that came down from heaven (John 6:31-35) and, secondly, because it signified Christ, who is the true bread from heaven. They actually ate the same spiritual bread we eat, they in type and we by faith.

vv.4, 5. 'They all drank the same water from a spiritual rock that followed them, and **that Rock was Christ**' in type and picture. Paul is saying to the Corinthians that all of Israel in wilderness days were an informed people, a privileged people, a people who were partakers of things that revealed the gospel of redemption in Christ, and yet the people who enjoyed those privileges were not pleasing to God nor accepted of him, but perished in the wilderness. This is a solemn warning (Heb. 3:6-14).

v.6. These people are an example to us who enjoy the blessed privilege and revelation of the gospel. The punishment inflicted upon them was designed as instruction for us to avoid the like sins, that we may not equally be condemned. The word 'lust' is to covet, crave, or desire and may be used in reference to all sin, for lust is the root and foundation of all sin (Rom. 7:7; 1 John 2:15, 16).

v. 7.   'Do not be worshippers of idols, images and false gods, as some of them were' (Exod. 32:1-6). Three thousand of them fell that day (Exod. 32:28). Our God is one God, is a jealous God and will not share his glory nor the love and worship of his people.

v. 8.   We must not gratify evil, fleshly desires and indulge in immorality, as some of these people did, which resulted in the death of twenty-four thousand (suddenly) one day (Num. 25:1-9; 1 Cor. 6:15-20).

v. 9.   'To tempt', in the general sense of the term, is to make a trial of God in reference to his power, his faithfulness and his goodness — to try his patience and be critical of his providence. It is not to be satisfied with his will and way, but to challenge him and provoke him. This Israel did in Numbers 21:5, 6.

v. 10.   'Murmuring' signifies speaking against God out of impatience, discontent or covetousness. We learn from Exodus 15:24; 16:7 and Numbers 14:26-29 that it was a sin of which the Jews were very much guilty.

v. 11.   These recorded punishments came upon Israel, not by chance, but by the will of God (as their idolatry and murmuring deserved) and were recorded for our admonition, that we may be warned to avoid the one and escape the other. Israel, blessed above all nations, presumed upon the goodness of God and suffered. We who live in the latter days before Christ's second coming are warned against such an attitude.

v. 12.   Since the Jewish fathers (who enjoyed such special favours and great privileges) by their sin, idolatry and rebellion brought upon themselves the judgements of God, it would be wise for all today (who think themselves safe, secure and above these sins) to take heed lest they also fall (Gal. 6:1; Jude 24). Our strength is not in ourselves or our knowledge, but totally in Christ (John 15:5).

v. 13. The word 'trial' may include trials such as afflictions, divine testing and all things disagreeable to nature (James 1:2; 1 Peter 1:6), or temptations that arise because of our sinful natures. These are all common to believers everywhere. We do not expect to be free from the common trials of all men. But God has promised strength and assistance to his people (Matt. 7:11; 2 Thess. 3:3). You may be tempted beyond your strength but not beyond his!

Do all to the glory of God

1 Corinthians 10 : 14-33

v. 14. **'Flee from idolatry'** of any sort, which is particularly offensive to our Lord! Not only avoid the worship of idols and the acts of idolatry, but believers should avoid that which gives even the appearance of idolatry, such as eating things offered to idols in an idol's temple. That this is what he especially had in mind we can judge from the following verses.

v. 15. Whereas he was speaking to intelligent, sensible men, he gave three arguments against associating themselves with idolaters in their temples of worship and eating with them at their feasts.

v. 16. The first argument is taken from *the Lord's Table.* When we sit at the Lord's Table and drink the wine and eat the bread, it suggests that we have a blessed union and communion with Christ. In like manner, when a man sits in an idol's temple and eats meat sacrificed to that idol, it indicates to all that he has a communion with that idol.

v. 17. The second argument is taken from *the believer's union and communion in Christ with one another.* No matter how numerous we are or whether we be Jew or Gentile, when

we meet around the table of the Lord, we are saying that we
are one body, one bread, one hope. In like manner, those who
associate with idolaters and eat their sacrificial meat give the
appearance, at least, of being one with idolaters.

v. 18.   The third argument is taken from *the Jewish nation.*
When they ate the flesh of sacrifices offered upon God's altar,
did they not by that act manifest that they were members of
God's assembly, that they believed in the God of the altar and
that they accepted this way of worship? In like manner, eating
sacrificial meat in an idol's temple indicates the owning of that
idol and a participation in the altar of idols.

vv. 19, 20.   What is Paul saying? That an idol has any reality
at all or that these sacrifices offered to them have any meaning?
Certainly not! But these pagan sacrifices are offered (in effect)
to demons and not to God. The nature of idolatry is to turn
from the living God to the creature, to will-worship, to idols,
and this is instigated, promoted and directed by devils, which
makes any worship, except true worship of the living God, to
be devil-worship! 'I do not want you to fellowship or have
anything to do with diabolical spirits' (Deut. 32:16, 17).

v. 21.   It is impossible to sit at both tables, to recognize the
true God and a false god, to live in two bodies, or to trust in
the sacrifice of Christ and the sacrifices to idols.

v. 22.   'Are we foolish enough to provoke the Lord to
jealousy, anger and indignation? (Exod. 20:3-5; 34:12-14.)
Do we think that we are stronger than he, that we should defy
him? How foolish!'

vv. 23, 24.   'Many things are lawful for me which are not wise.
Many things which are not sinful in themselves may be
detrimental to me and to others. What is permissible is not
always advisable. What I *can* do, without sinning, is not always
what I *should* do!
    Let us not then seek our own pleasure, profit and advantage,

but the welfare and good of others. "Love seeketh not her own." '

vv. 25-28. 'When you go to the market or butcher's shop and meat offered to idols is sold in common with other meat, it may be bought and eaten with no questions asked, because the earth and all that is in it are the Lord's, and his people have a right to it through him. If an unbeliever invites you to eat with him, you may eat what is set before you, so long as no issue is raised about the meat's being from the idol's temple. Nor must you inquire about the source from which the meat was secured.

However, if someone tells you, "This is meat from the idol's temple," do not eat it. Do not eat it for the sake of the one who made the point and for the sake of a weak brother who may be offended. There is plenty of other food without it.'

vv. 29-31. 'Why should my way of life be determined by another man's conscience? Why should my behaviour be guided by another man's principles? Why should I allow my liberty to be suppressed by another man's weakness? If I am guided by the Scriptures and give thanks for all that I have or do, why should I be criticized? The whole matter is resolved in this: whatever I eat, drink, or do, I must consider first the glory of God!'

vv. 32, 33. 'If I have the glory of God as my chief concern, I will be careful not to offend needlessly the Jews, the Gentiles, nor the church of God.' Paul gives himself as an example in these things. He was careful not to seek only to please himself, but made every effort not to hinder others in order that they might come to know Christ.

The head of the woman is the man

1 Corinthians 11 : 1-16

v.1.   The apostle exhorts the Corinthians to follow his
teachings, his example and his advice only as he followed the
teachings and commandments of Christ. The words of our
Lord are our only certain rule of faith and practice. Our
ministers and leaders are only to be obeyed and followed as
they teach and practise the teachings of Christ.

v.2.   He praised them that, even in his absence, they remem-
bered his ministry and kept the doctrines, traditions and
instructions that he had delivered to them when he was among
them.

v.3.   Christ is the head of every individual human being
(John 17:2; Rom. 14:9; Matt. 28:18), but in this sense we
understand 'every man' to mean every member of his body,
the church (Col. 1:18). 'The head of the woman is the man'
(Gen. 3:16; 1 Cor. 14:34, 35; Eph. 5:22-24). 'The head of
Christ is God,' not as to his divine nature, for in that respect
they are one! Christ is equal to the Father and is possessed of
the same divine perfections; but in respect of his office as
Mediator, the Son is come to do the will of the Father. In
Christ there is neither male nor female in respect of essence,
nature and position; but as to office, leadership and authority
in the church and in the home, the woman is in subjection and
under the rule of the man (1 Tim. 2:11, 12).

vv.4-6.   Interpreters rightly agree that this and the following
verses are to be interpreted in the light of the customs of
countries as long as the principles of the Scriptures are not
violated or compromised. In those Eastern countries it signified

either shame or subjection for a person to be 'veiled' or 'covered'. A woman never appeared in public without a covering on her head and a veil over her face. If she did, it was an act of rebellion against authority and a demand for equality socially with men. This is not true in our generation where being bare-headed speaks of subjection and being covered betokens superiority and dominion! For a man in Corinth to pray or worship with a covering on his head would indicate that he recognized some human head or authority other than Christ and would be dishonouring to Christ, who is the only head of men. For a woman in Corinth to take off her covering in prayer and worship would indicate that she did not agree with her part in the Fall, nor the authority of her husband over her, nor the commandment of God to be in subjection. This would dishonour her husband and would be as shameful as if she had shaved her head. For her to appear in the dress and manner of her superior would indicate her rebellion against God's order.

vv. 7, 8. The sexes should not attempt to change places. The order in which God has placed persons is best, and to endeavour to change it is to introduce confusion (Deut. 22:5). The woman should keep to the rank God has chosen for her. She was made out of man, made for man and made to be the glory of man. She should always conduct herself according to this divine plan in the home and in the church.

The man was first made and made head of the creation here below, and therein he is the image or representative of God's dominion. The woman was made out of the man to be his helpmeet, to be in subjection to him, and therein she is the glory of her husband and his representative. A woman's attitude and behaviour are a reflection of her husband, either for glory or for shame.

v. 9. Man was not created for woman, to be ruled by her nor for her benefit, but woman was made for man's use, help and comfort, and naturally made subject to him (Gen. 2:18, 22, 25; Eph. 5:22-25).

v.10. A woman should behave in such a way (in this case and country the veil was considered the symbol of subjection) as to show her subjection because of the presence of angels. Some say these are the evil angels. The woman was first in the transgression, being deceived by the evil angel, Lucifer (1 Tim. 2:14; 2 Cor. 11:3), and the presence of evil spirits among us would capitalize on a woman's effort to again usurp authority. Others say these are the elect angels who minister to and among us (Heb. 1:14), who would be grieved.

vv.11, 12. Nevertheless, lest this order of the sexes be carried too far and men become overbearing, harsh and independent of women, and women become slaves without spirit, lose their spiritual interest and initiative and hesitate to witness, pray and serve the Lord, Paul declares men and women need each other! They were made to be a mutual comfort and blessing to one another in the Lord (1 Peter 3:5-7). As woman was first formed out of man, the man is ever since born of woman, nourished and comforted by her.

vv.13-15. 'Consult your own reason; listen to what nature teaches. Should there not be a distinction kept up between the sexes? The man — the leader, the provider, strong and masculine; the woman — in subjection, feminine, with longer hair, which is a natural sign of her character and person. But for a man to dress or wear his hair as a woman is a token of softness and effeminacy.' It should be our concern in our assemblies to break no rules of natural distinction.

v.16. 'Now if anyone is disposed to be contentious about this matter, let him know that the apostles and all the churches hold this position.'

The Lord's Table

1 Corinthians 11 : 17-34

In this passage Paul rebukes the church for their conduct in respect to the observance of the Lord's Table. We are told by ancient writers that in some of the early churches observance of the Lord's Table was preceded with a love feast which led to some improper behaviour.

vv.17, 18. 'In the matter I will deal with now, I do not praise you but must condemn you; for when you meet together to observe this ordinance, you are doing more harm than good. You are not edifying and instructing; but rather you are indulging the flesh in intemperance, causing division, factions and even heresies.'

v.19. There will always be divisions, factions and heresies in churches because Satan is always busy sowing tares, false prophets and teachers are plentiful and human nature (being weak and wicked) is easily led astray. These things do not come forth by chance but through the providence of God, who allows Satan to show himself and allows men to discover the evil of their own hearts in order that those who are genuine (whose doctrine and conduct are according to Scripture) might be recognized plainly.

vv.20, 21. 'When you gather together for your love feasts and so-called observance of the Lord's Supper, it is not the supper instituted by our Lord that you observe.' According to some writers, as Christ did eat the Passover supper before the Lord's Supper, in an imitation of a sort, they would prepare lavish meals at home and bring them to the meeting-place. Some had much to eat, some had little or none, some even

drank too much wine and none of them shared with, or waited
for others. These love feasts turned into unlovely debaucheries.

v. 22. 'Do you not have private homes in which to eat, drink
and indulge your appetites? Do you have contempt for the
place where the church meets? Do you have contempt for the
poor people of the church, who are not blessed as you are?'
It is a good thing for a church to bring food, come together for
fellowship, equally sharing and waiting one for the other in
feasts of love and fellowship, but certainly not in conjunction
with the observance of the Lord's Table.

vv. 23-26.   Paul then sets forth the Lord's Table as it should
be observed by the Lord's church.
   1. He tells how he came by the knowledge of it — by
revelation from Christ!
   2. He sets forth the Author of it — the Lord Jesus himself!
   3. He gives the time of the institution — the same night he
was betrayed and arrested.
   4. He lists the materials of the supper — bread and wine
(Luke 22:14-20). The bread represented his body, broken, and
the wine his blood, which was shed for us. Nothing is said of
the absurd doctrine of transubstantiation. The bread and wine
do not actually become the body and blood of the Lord, but
only represent or symbolize his body and blood. **'This do in
remembrance of me,'** said our Lord, in order to keep fresh in
our minds and hearts his sacrifice for our sins and his intercession now on our behalf. We not only remember his death for
us, but we 'show', declare, or proclaim his substitutionary
work (1 Peter 1:18, 19).
   5. It should be observed frequently, no time is specified;
but, 'As often as you observe the table, you remember and
proclaim his death.'

vv. 27-29.   Whoever eats the Lord's Table in a way that is
unworthy of Christ may be said to be guilty of the body
and blood of Christ, insomuch as he violates this important
ordinance, despises the precious blood of Christ and treats

lightly the sufferings of our Lord. Let each person examine himself concerning his own knowledge of Christ – who Christ is, what Christ did, why Christ suffered and where Christ is now. Let him determine his experience concerning repentance, faith and love for the Redeemer; then let him eat. For an unworthy person (not a believer) to come to the table, or for him to come in an unworthy manner (as the Corinthians were doing), or to come for an unworthy purpose is to bring God's wrath upon himself! This is no ordinary supper, but a most holy time.

v. 30. Because of their unworthy treatment of the Lord's Table, God had visited some of them with afflictions and even death.

vv. 31, 32. 'If we will examine ourselves, as directed in the above verses, confess our sins, condemn ourselves and look to Christ alone for forgiveness through his blood, we will not come under divine judgement (1 John 1:9; 2:1, 2). But when we are under the trying hand of the Lord, let us be comforted to know that God deals with us as a Father disciplines, corrects and instructs his children, so that we shall not finally be condemned with the world of unbelievers.

vv. 33, 34. 'When you gather together to observe the Lord's Table, meet together as one body, wait for one another. If anyone is hungry, let him eat at home.' This is not a time to satisfy fleshly appetites, but a time of worship and remembrance of our Lord.

The nature and use of spiritual gifts

1 Corinthians 12 : 1-14

v.1.   The church at Corinth evidently abounded in special,
God-given spiritual gifts, such as wisdom, knowledge, faith,
healing, miracles, prophecy, discerning of spirits, tongues and
the interpretation of tongues. Some were discouraged because
they did not have these gifts, others were elated and puffed up
by their offices and abilities, and some abused and misused
them. Paul writes concerning the Author of gifts, the excellency
of them and the nature and true use of them, and says, 'I don't
want you to be misinformed about this matter.'

v.2.   'None of you has any reason to be proud or lifted up
with your knowledge and gifts. God found you in heathen
idolatry; so that, if you are favoured with any spiritual wisdom
or gift, it is owing to his grace, not to your merit (1 Cor. 4:6, 7).
Let us ascribe all to the free grace of God and be humble
under a sense of unworthiness.

v.3.   Every believer has the Holy Spirit, who regenerated us,
called us, sanctified us and who indwells us (Rom. 8:9; 1 Cor.
2:12). Whether we have unusual gifts or not, we have the
Spirit of God, evidenced by the fact that we acknowledge with
our lips, hearts and lives that Jesus Christ is King of kings and
Lord of lords. No man has this knowledge or confesses this
truth except under the power and influence of the Spirit of
God (John 16:13-15).

v.4.   There are different gifts; none have all, but all have
some and, while we are not all alike, it is the same Holy Spirit
who gives gifts and graces as he pleases (vv.11, 18). Let those
who have much be humbled and let those who have little be
thankful.

v.5. There are different offices or ministries in the church. One ministers as pastor, another as elder, another as deacon, another in this or that capacity; but all serve the same great Lord of the church. It is his church, his vineyard and his will that we seek.

v.6. There are different effects, workings, or accomplishments (2 Cor. 2:14-16), but it is the same God who uses us, when he will, where he will and in the way that he will.

v. 7. The gifts, offices and operations of the Spirit are not to make gain of (like Simon Magus), nor to encourage pride and envy, nor to cause division, but for the glory of God and the profit and good of the whole church.

vv. 8-10. In these verses Paul identifies some of these spiritual gifts.

1. **'The word of wisdom'** — a knowledge of the mysteries of the gospel and the ability to explain them. It might also mean good judgement in decisions.

2. **'The word of knowledge'** — a universal knowledge of Scriptures wrapped up in the types, prophecies and doctrines of the Word (1 Cor. 2:12, 13).

3. **'Faith'** — the faith of miracles, or faith in the divine power and promises, whereby they are enabled to work miracles.

4. **'The gifts of healing'** — the healing of the sick, either by laying on of hands, or anointing with oil, or with a word.

5. **'The working of miracles'** — power to give sight to the blind, hearing to the deaf, or even to raise the dead.

6. **'Prophecy'** — the ability to foretell future events or to explain Scripture.

7. **'Discerning of spirits'** — power to distinguish between true and false prophets, or to discern what is of God and what is of Satan.

8. **'Tongues'** — ability to speak the gospel in a language they had not learned.

9. **'Interpretation of tongues'** — when a discourse was delivered in another language, some had the power to interpret it to the people.

v.11.   These gifts and abilities are given by the Holy Spirit, not to all believers, but one gift to this man, another gift to another man, as the Holy Spirit pleases. He is sovereign in the distribution of gifts and grace.

v.12.   The human body has many parts, such as hands, feet, ears and eyes. As numerous and different as these members are, they are, nevertheless, parts of the same body. They make up one body. So it is with the church, the body of Christ.

v.13.   Whether we be Jews or Gentiles, bond or free, old or young, male or female, every believer has been baptized into the body of Jesus Christ. Christ is the Head and we are his body. We are all partakers of one Spirit, one life, and one goal — the exaltation and glory of Jesus Christ (Col. 1:16-18; 1 Cor. 10:17).

v.14.   **'The body is not one member'**, however important, such as the eye, the ear, or the arm. The body consists of many members, different but necessary to form a complete body. So the body of Christ is not one person nor one sort of person; but there are many members, some in a high station, some low; some of great gifts, some less; some Jew and some Gentile; but all are one in Christ and all are related to, and needful of the others.

The body of Christ - the church

1 Corinthians 12 : 15-31

vv.15, 16.   It appears from this statement that these special
spiritual gifts, offices and operations had caused divisions in
the church. Some of the members felt inferior, unnecessary
and slighted, because they were not gifted and did not have a
prominent ministry. Others who preached, taught, or were
especially gifted looked down upon those who did not have
certain gifts and abilities. This is unreasonable, says the apostle,
for the body is not made up of only one member, but many
members, all different but all performing their necessary duties.
The foot is not a hand and does not serve in the same manner,
but it is necessary to the body's function. The ear is not an
eye, but it is as necessary as the eye!

v.17.   What if every believer were a preacher? There would
be no hearers! If every believer were an organist, there would
be no singers! If every believer were an elder, there would be
no custodian! If every believer were an overseer, there would
be no workers, no givers, no teachers, no children! If everyone
were young and zealous, there would be no patient counsel
which only experience and age can provide.

vv.18-20.   The infinitely wise God made the body of man
and put every member of man's body where it is, doing what it
does for the proper functioning of the body. So the Lord has
put us, as members, in his mystical body, the church, in such a
place and part as it pleased him. Every member ought to be
content with his place, gift and usefulness because it is God's
will for him and because, without all of the necessary members,
there would be no body. Now we are different in parts, places,
gifts and service, but one body in Christ!

v. 21.   The eye is vital to the body's well-being, but it cannot say to the hand, 'I have no need of you.' Nor can the head say to the foot, 'Because you are a lowly member which does not speak, reason, or hear, I do not need you.' *Every member* is of use to the whole body.

v. 22.   Actually those parts of the body such as the liver, intestines and stomach, which are not displayed, recognized, or talked about, are as necessary to the body's life and usefulness as any other part. Even so, all believers in the church, the strong and the weak, the recognized and the unrecognized, the leaders and the followers, are necessary (2 Cor. 12:9, 10).

v. 23.   There are parts of the human body which are considered less comely and less honourable, which we do not expose to the public, but upon which we bestow honour and recognition, for we clothe them carefully and attractively; and to us they are important and beautiful as God's creation. So, in the church body, let those who appear less honourable and less out-going be clothed with love, grace and kindness.

v. 24.   Our eyes, ears, hands and faces have no need of special adornment or attention, for they are constantly seen, honoured and cared for. But don't forget or neglect those other parts of the body without which we have no life. God has composed the church in such a way that all members are beneficial and necessary to the life of the church, and he bestows his honour and glory to all equally (1 Cor. 1:26-29). He will humble the gifted and lift up the lowly.

vv. 25-27.   By 'schism' is meant division. Though members differ in office, honour, gifts, personality, etc., yet all should have the same care and love for each other as though they were of equal importance, for, indeed, they are. When one member suffers, all suffer with him; when one member is honoured, all rejoice. As with the human body, a broken arm is felt by the whole body. We are members of the body of Christ, therefore we are one body joined together. How can we not be affected by the pain or rejoicing of a part of ourselves?

vv. 28-30. In his sovereign purpose God has given to the church apostles, prophets, teachers, men and women with this gift and that gift, with this ability and that ability. Are they all the same? Are they all alike? No more than the human body can be all eyes, or ears, or hands. There must be the presence of all organs, faculties and members to make a human body; so there must be many different members in the body of Christ.

v. 31. This verse must be joined with the first verse of chapter 13, so will be covered in the next lesson.

The greatest of these is love

1 Corinthians 13 : 1-13

At the close of the last chapter Paul exhorted the Corinthians to desire the best spiritual gifts for the glory of God, the preaching of the gospel and the good of the whole church. But there is something better than supernatural gifts! There is something to be desired more than knowledge, unusual spiritual talents and offices, and that is true, sincere, heart love to God and men.

v. 1. 'If I could speak with the tongues or languages of every nation on earth and express myself as the angels do, yet have not that God-given (Rom. 5:5; 1 John 4:7, 8), heart-felt brotherly love (a true root of love for men which flows from a true love for God), I only make an irritating noise with my mouth, which will be of no use to me or to others.'

v. 2. 'If I had the gift of prophecy, whereby I could preach the mysteries of Scripture and even foretell the purpose of God in reference to the future, and though I have a vast

knowledge of the most sublime and hidden things and a **faith** of miracles to accomplish most unusual things (Matt. 17:20), **if I have not this brotherly love, I am nothing!'** I may be great in the eyes of men, but in the account of God, *I am nothing!*

v.3. **'If I give away all my possessions to feed the poor.'** Why would a man do this if he did not love the poor? He might, like Ananias and Sapphira (Acts 5:1-5), or the Pharisee (Luke 18:11, 12), do it for praise and self-righteous purposes. **If I give my body to be burned,'** or die as a martyr for the cause of orthodoxy and religion, **'it will all profit me nothing!'** No actions, no human sacrifice and no human sufferings are sufficient to entitle any soul to heaven. If I have not love for Christ and for men, all of these gifts, offices and self-righteous efforts are vain and useless! Love is the *commandment of Christ* (John 15:12). Love is the *evidence of salvation* (John 13:35). Love is the *fruit of the indwelling Spirit* (Gal. 5:22). Love is so essential that, if a man has everything else and has not love, he is nothing. Love is not the prerogative of a few; it must be the possession of all.

v.4. **'Love suffers long,'** that is, it makes a man patient and long-suffering with the faults of others. He is not easily offended and given to wrath. **Love is kind,** tender and compassionate. Love wishes to bestow the best that it can on the object of its affection (Eph. 4:32). **Love envieth not,** or does not boil over with jealousy, but is made happy by the prosperity and happiness of others. Nothing is more adverse to love than envy. **Love vaunteth not itself**; it is never proud, conceited, or arrogant. What do we have to be conceited about? 'Who maketh thee to differ?' (1 Cor. 4:7.) **'Love is not puffed up!'** (Rom. 12:3, 10.)

v.5. **'Love is not rude and unmannerly.'** Pride, conceit and self-righteousness beget rudeness, but love produces humility and courtesy. **'Love seeketh not her own way,'** rights and will (Phil. 2:3-8). **'Love is not easily provoked.'** Love is not touchy, resentful, easily offended. **'Love thinketh no evil.'** It does not

carry about a suspicious nature looking for faults, but rather it
thinks the best of others.

v.6. **'Love rejoices not in the fall and failure of others, but
rejoices in goodness and truth.'** Love is never glad when others
go wrong. What a man is, he wishes others to be. If he is evil,
he delights to point to evil in others.

v.7. **'Love beareth all things.'** The word is 'Love covers with
silence all things' (Prov. 10:12; 11:13; 17:9). **'Love believeth
all things'** (James 3:14-18). It is better to believe the best of a
brother and be disappointed than to believe the worst and
destroy a friendship. **'Love hopeth all things.'** What love
cannot see, it hopes for; it never gives up! **'Love endureth all
things.'** It will endure trial, sorrow, sickness, disappointment,
hurt feelings and offence.

vv.8, 9. **'Love never fails.'** It will endure to the end. It never
ceases in this life nor in the life to come. It is of God, the gift
of God and the life of God in a man (Eccles. 3:14). Someday
the gifts of prophecy, tongues, healings and even knowledge
shall vanish away, for we only know in part and prophesy in
part. So much of divine mysteries and knowledge is unknown
to us, but love goes on in glory. The most knowledgeable and
gifted man is but a babe. But love is love and will grow, but
not be superseded.

vv.10-12. When perfect knowledge of God, of Christ, and of
the mysteries of the kingdom of heaven shall be ours in heaven,
our imperfect knowledge, our weak faith, our so-called
excellent gifts and rare talents will appear to be but children's
toys in the sight of what we shall know and be.
  'When I reached manhood, I put away my childish toys,
thoughts and behaviour'; even so, when believers shall see
Christ and be like him (perfect, mature saints), tongues shall
cease, prophecies shall fail, limited knowledge shall vanish
away.

v. 13.   There are three main graces — **faith,** by which we look
to Christ, receive Christ and live upon him; **hope,** by which we
wait for the fulfilment of every promise in Christ and **love** to
God and all men — yet love exceeds the others as to its duration
and use. Faith shall give way to sight, hope to reality; but love
shall only expand.

Speaking in other languages

1 Corinthians 14 : 1-17

In this chapter the apostle writes concerning the right use of
spiritual gifts and prefers prophesying, or preaching, to every
other gift.

v. 1.   '**Follow after** that **love** to God and toward your brethren
about which I have been speaking. Make love your aim, and at
the same time **covet spiritual gifts.**' Because love has the
pre-eminence does not mean that we are to despise or neglect
these gifts (2 Tim. 1:6; 1 Tim. 4:13, 14). Of all the gifts, the
gift of preaching the Word (the ability to open the Scriptures
and the gift to explain the Old Testament prophecies, promises
and types fulfilled in Christ) is of the greatest value to the
church.

v. 2.   The word 'unknown' is not in the original Scriptures. It
has been supplied by the translators. By a '**tongue**' Paul means
a language not known or understood by most of the hearers.
Suppose a person has the gift to speak or preach in another
language (Acts 2:4-8) and, whether to show off his gift or
for whatever reason, he uses that language to speak to the
congregation. He speaks not to them, for they do not understand him. God understands him, for he is the Author of all
languages. He may preach, under the influence of the Holy
Spirit, great and wonderful mysteries, but it is of no profit,
for no one understands him.

v. 3. He who preaches to men the gospel of Christ in the common language *edifies* men. There is an increase in knowledge and understanding. He *exhorts* them to walk in faith, obedience and holiness. He *comforts* the people of God who are troubled and burdened. God gives a blessing through the preached Word, but the blessing cannot come through a language not understood (Rom. 10:13-15; 1 John 5:20).

v. 4. He that speaks in a language not known by the hearers may warm his own heart and bless his own soul (if he understands what he is saying), but he that preaches in an intelligible language and style is a blessing to all who hear him.

v. 5. Evidently all did not have this extraordinary gift of the Spirit to speak in a language they never learned, and Paul says he would be happy if they did have it. However, more than this, he rather wished that they all had the ability to open and apply the Scriptures to men's understanding; for he who preaches and teaches the Word of God in a man's own tongue is more useful and important than the man who speaks in an unknown tongue, unless he interprets what he says, that the people might be edified.

v. 6. 'Suppose I come to you speaking in a language you do not understand. What good would it do you? Unless there is a revelation of Christ to the heart, a knowledge of our sins, his mercy and his will of redemption, a telling forth of his purpose in Christ and the doctrines of grace, my ministry among you would be fruitless.' Men cannot believe what they do not hear.

vv. 7-9. When a person plays a musical instrument, he must play certain notes which are set in order according to a prescribed time, or no one will know the song he is playing. The trumpet was used by armies to sound charge or retreat. How will the soldiers know whether to charge or to fall back if there is no clear, understandable note sounded?

'So it is with preaching or teaching. If you speak in a language no one understands, he will not know what you are saying. You will just be talking into the air.'

vv.10, 11.   The whole earth was originally of one language (Gen. 11:1); but God gave them many languages (Gen. 11:7), so that now there are many tongues and languages, and the words in all languages are significant to those who understand them.

Therefore, if the language is not known to both speaker and hearer, they will be like foreigners to one another.

v.12.   The Corinthians were very ambitious of spiritual gifts; therefore, Paul advises them to concentrate on seeking those gifts and the proper use of them so that the church may be edified. 'Seek to excel and abound in gifts for the glory of God and the good of the church.'

v.13.   In 1 Corinthians 12:10 and 30 it appears that the gift to speak in tongues and the gift to interpret were distinct. Evidently a man could have one without the other. A man may be able to preach in another language and yet not be capable of translating it into the common language of the people. Therefore, if one speaks in another language, let him pray for the ability to interpret what he has said.

vv.14, 15.   'If I pray in the assembly in an unknown language (whether I understand, as some think, or do not understand, as others think), my spirit (by the Holy Spirit within me) does truly pray. But it bears no fruit and helps nobody if no one understands me, nor does it edify me if I do not understand.

What is to be done then? Here is the reply: 'I will pray with the influence and aid of the Spirit of God, but I will also pray in a language that I myself and others may understand what I say.' The same thing is applicable to what we sing.

vv. 16, 17. 'If you praise God and render thanks led by the Holy Spirit, how can the man who does not understand what you are saying worship with you and say "Amen" to your prayer? You give thanks and are blessed, but he is not edified.'

Worship in an orderly fashion

1 Corinthians 14 : 18-40

vv. 18, 19. Paul lets them know that he did not despise the gift of tongues, nor did he discourage them from desiring the gift nor using it. He had this gift and used it in the many countries to which he travelled and preached. He could speak in more different languages than anyone, yet he says that he had rather speak a few words to the congregation in a language they understand than ten thousand words in a language no one understands. If men understand our words, we can communicate to them the doctrines of the gospel and the mysteries of grace.

v. 20. There are some things in which it is commendable to be like little children. Children are usually tender-hearted, ready to forgive, willing to be taught, free from pride and vain glory and without guile and hypocrisy. 'But in your thinking and judgement, don't act like babies; act like mature men.' His chief reference here is to the way they were acting in this matter of gifts, behaving with childish vanity and immaturity!

v. 21. There is no reason to be over-excited about speaking the Word of God in other languages, for in Isaiah 28:11, 12 the Lord says, 'By men of strange languages and by lips of foreigners I will speak to these people (in their own tongue — Acts 2:5-8) and not even then will they listen to me.' Men are not converted by signs and wonders but by the Spirit and the Word (Luke 16:29-31).

v. 22. The power of the apostles and other early preachers to speak supernaturally in other languages is not a sign for believers (who need no miracle to gain their attention or to confirm their faith), but these gifts and miracles bore witness before unbelievers that these men were sent from God and preached a message from heaven (Heb. 2:3, 4; John 3:2). Inspired preaching and teaching (interpreting the divine will and purpose of God in Christ) serves to edify believers – not unbelievers, who must first be regenerated and given ears to hear.

v. 23. 'If the church be assembled together and all of you are speaking in whatever tongues and languages you are gifted to speak and one comes in who is unlearned and untaught in the things of the Spirit, he will think you are all crazy.'

vv. 24, 25. 'But if you preach the Word in the Spirit and with the understanding, and people are present who are unbelievers, yet who understand your words, it may be that they shall hear the Word of God, be convinced of sin, be brought to see the glorious gospel of Christ and fall on their faces in worship and faith, declaring that God is among you in very truth.'

vv. 26-35. 'What then is the right and proper order of using these gifts which you have? When you come together in the assembly and different ones have different gifts and abilities, how shall they all be used for the glory of God and the good of the church? All things must be done for edification, instruction and the good of all.'

1. If men speak in another language, limit the speakers to two or three, with each taking his turn while another interprets what he says.

2. If there is no one present who can interpret what is said, let the person keep silent in the assembly and speak quietly to himself and God.

3. Let two or three preachers, who are gifted to teach or preach, speak in the service while the rest pay attention, weigh and discern what is said.

4. If a man is inspired of God to speak, if a message is laid on his heart, then let him wait until the first one is silent, or let the first one be silent and allow him to speak.

5. We are not to sing, preach, or pray all at the same time, but one by one, to avoid confusion and disorder. Men cannot learn or be comforted in disorder and confusion.

6. The gifts, abilities and talents a man has are subject to the man's wisdom and should be controlled by him. God is not the author of confusion, but he is the author of peace, order and wisdom. If a man cannot use his gifts in a sane, orderly fashion for God's glory and the good of all, it is a sign that the Spirit of God is not in him.

7. What has been said before does not apply to women, for they are to keep silent in the assembly. Women are not authorized to teach, preach, nor usurp and exercise authority over the men in the church. If they have a problem to be resolved or a question to be answered, let them have it resolved by their husbands at home (1 Tim. 2:11, 12). This is what the Old Testament teaches also (Gen. 3:16).

vv. 36-38. Here is a sharp rebuke to those in Corinth who thought themselves wise, spiritually grown and beyond the instructions of the apostle Paul. He asks, 'Did the gospel originate with you? Did the Word of God come to you only?' There were churches in Jerusalem and in other places before there was a church at Corinth. 'If one among you is lifted up with pride and claims to be a prophet and spiritually wise, he must acknowledge that I am an apostle and what I am writing to you is the command of the Lord. But if any man refuses to own these words to be the commandment of Christ, let him be treated as an ignorant man, shunned and rejected.'

vv. 39, 40. 'Wherefore, brethen, desire to preach and teach the Word. Do not despise nor forbid men to speak in other languages if they are so gifted, but let all things be done decently and in an orderly fashion.'

The resurrection of the dead - I

1 Corinthians 15 : 1-19

In this chapter the apostle proves the resurrection of Christ
and with different arguments he establishes the resurrection of
all men. Evidently another problem that had risen in the church
was the denial by some of the resurrection (v.12; 2 Tim. 2:17,
18). The doctrine of the resurrection is a fundamental article
of the gospel; without it we have no gospel (v.17; 2 Tim. 2:8).
Much of the wrath and persecution that came upon the
apostles from the Sadducees, the Jews, the philosophers and
the Gentiles was because they preached the resurrection
(Acts 17:31, 32; 24:14, 15, 21).

v.1. 'Let me remind you, brethren (since it seems to have
escaped some of you), of **the gospel which I preached unto
you** when I first came among you. This is the gospel **which
you received** with faith and joy — the gospel **in which and for
which** most of **you stand**, though some of you have been
seduced and warped by false teachers' (Gal. 1:6-9).

v.2. 'By believing and receiving the gospel of Christ, you are
saved. The gospel is the power of God unto salvation (Rom.
1:16; Mark 16:15,16), but not unless you persevere (keep in
memory what I preached) and continue in the faith of the
gospel (Col. 1:21-23; Heb. 3:6, 13, 14). Unless you continue
in faith, your profession (your so-called faith) is all in vain'
(1 John 2:19).

vv.3, 4. '**I delivered** (or preached) **unto you what I received**
from our Lord himself (Gal. 1:11, 12), **how that Christ**, the
Messiah, the Anointed One, **died** that he might satisfy divine
justice **for our sins** (Rom. 3:25, 26; Isa. 53:4-6), was buried

and rose again the third day, and all of his work on our behalf was **according to the Old Testament Scriptures**. Every promise, prophecy and type recorded in the Law and the Prophets concerning the Messiah had its fulfilment in Jesus of Nazareth (Luke 24:27, 44, 45). The Old Testament contained the New Testament in picture and prophecy, and the New Testament is the Old Testament fully and plainly revealed (Acts 10:43).

vv. 5-7. In these verses Paul calls forth the eye-witnesses of the resurrected Lord. The Scriptures say, 'In the mouth of two or three witnesses shall every word be established' (2 Cor. 13:1). The Lord appeared to Simon Peter, then to the Twelve. (Though Judas was dead, they went by their original name, the Twelve — John 20:24.) Later Christ showed himself to more than five hundred brethren at one time (Matt. 28:16, 17). 'Most of these people who saw him are still alive,' Paul said, 'but some are dead,' for this epistle was written twenty-six years later. He appeared to James and then again to all the disciples when he was taken up into heaven (Acts 1:1-3, 9, 10).

v. 8. The last appearance of the risen Lord was fo Paul (Acts 9:3, 4). To be an apostle one must have been an eye-witness of the glory of Christ and must have received his gospel directly from Christ. Paul had both credentials. His revelation of Christ came after the others (after Christ had risen and ascended) as an abortive birth or one born at the wrong time. His sight of Christ was not according to the pattern established with the other apostles.

v. 9. **'I am the least of the apostles,'** not in office, dignity, gifts, or labour, but deserving the least esteem because he had not stood with the others in the early days but was (with the Pharisees) a persecutor of the name of Christ and the people of God (Acts 9:1-3).

v. 10. **'By the unmerited favour and blessings of God, I am what I am.'** Paul defends his authority and magnifies his office by declaring that these gifts and grace bestowed on him were

not fruitless and in vain, for he laboured more abundantly and
had more success than any of the others. Yet he is careful to
ascribe nothing to himself but all to the grace of God, which
enabled him both to believe and to serve God (1 Cor. 4:7;
John 3:26, 27).

v.11.   Therefore, it matters not whether they heard those
who saw Christ first or Paul, who saw him last. The subject
matter of their ministry was the same – namely, the incarnate,
suffering, risen Redeemer. Christ, not the preacher, is the
object of saving faith.

v.12.   If both the Old Testament and the New Testament
declare his resurrection, if the apostles (who were eye-witnesses
of his resurrection) preach the resurrection, if the gospel
declares the absolute necessity of Christ's resurrection, how is
it that some among you say there is no resurrection of the
dead? This is an absolute denial of the Scriptures, the gospel
and the word of Christ's apostles.

vv.13-19.   Then follow several severe consequences of such
teaching:
    1. **'If there is no resurrection of the dead, then Christ is not
risen.'** Christ became a man, died in the flesh and was buried.
If men do not live again, then he is not alive.
    2. **'If Christ be not risen, all of our preaching is in vain** and
amounts to nothing, and your faith in God is devoid of truth
and will profit you nothing.'
    3. 'We apostles and preachers have misrepresented God, for
**we have testified of God that he raised Christ from the dead,
whom he did not raise, if the dead rise not'** (Acts 2:23, 24, 32).
    4. He repeats for emphasis, **'If the dead are not raised, then
Christ is not raised.'** He is still in the tomb and proved to be an
impostor.
    5. 'Your object of faith, Christ, is not raised; therefore, **your
faith is worthless,** you are not saved, you know not God, you
have no mediator, and you are still in a state of unregeneracy
and guilt.'

6. 'Those of your number **who have died believing in Christ** and trusting him to save them **are perished** and eternally lost.'

7. The fashion of this world fades and believers in Christ are persecuted, hated and cast down. Our hope is not in this world but in the world to come. If these promises are not true, our hopes are in vain and **we are the most miserable** and frustrated **of all men.**

The resurrection of the dead - II

1 Corinthians 15 : 20-34

v.20.   The first-fruits were what first sprang out of the earth, were soonest ripe, were reaped first, gathered in and offered to the Lord (Deut. 26:1-3). So Christ first rose from the dead, ascended to heaven and presented himself to God as the representative of his people. There were others who were raised from the dead before him, but Christ was the first to be raised to immortal life. All of these others died again. He is the first-born from the dead, that in all things he might have the pre-eminence (Col. 1:18). Our resurrection is secured by him, our Representative (John 14:19).

vv.21, 22.   The first man, Adam, was the representative, the covenant and federal head of all men. We all lived in him and died in him when he sinned (Rom. 5:12). Sin, disease, physical death and eternal death came upon us through Adam's disobedience. So Christ is the Representative, the covenant and federal Head of the elect, and because he became a man, obeyed God's law perfectly, died for our sins and rose again, in him we have righteousness, redemption and eternal life (Rom. 5:17-19). All who are **'in Adam'** die; all who are **'in Christ'** (by grace, divine purpose and faith) shall live.

v.23.   God has appointed the order of the resurrection of his

people. Christ is the first-fruits of this harvest, rising from the
dead to die no more. Afterwards, at his second coming, all
believers shall rise together (1 Thess. 4:13-17; 1 John 3:2).

v. 24.   'Then cometh the end' – that is, the accomplishment,
completion and perfection of all things: the end of the world
as it now is; the end of all *evil power,* authority and activity;
the end of all *earthly rule,* authority and divisions, such as
nations, families and races; the end of all *ecclesiastical rule,*
authority and power. There will be no more prophets, apostles,
bishops and pastors and teachers. But the *mediatorial kingdom
of Christ* is referred to here mainly. The grand design of the
Father in creation, providence and salvation is to have a new
heaven and a new earth, wherein dwells righteousness, populated
by a holy people perfectly conformed to the likeness of his
Son. This he gave to Christ, in the eternal council and covenant,
to accomplish, to perfect and to deliver to him at the end
(Luke 22:37; John 17:4; 6:38, 39).

vv. 25, 26.   The Lord God has decreed that Christ should (as
Prophet, Priest and King) reign over his people, over all flesh
(John 17:2), over all things (Matt. 28:18; Col. 1:16-18;
Ps. 110:1), until every contrary creature, word, thought and
imagination are conquered. The last enemy to be destroyed
will be death, for we shall rise to die no more.

v. 27.   Paul refers to Psalm 8:4-6, and according to Hebrews
2:6-9, this is Christ. But the apostle adds that when God said,
'All things are put under his feet,' the Father is not included!

v. 28.   When all is accomplished, God's design in redemption
is complete and all evil is cast out, then nothing shall appear
but the essential kingdom of God, the power by which the
Father, Son and Holy Spirit (three persons though but one
God) shall reign.

v. 29.   The apostle returns to his subject, the resurrection of
the dead. 'If the dead are not raised, then why do we submit

to believers' baptism, which declares that we died with Christ, are buried and are risen with Christ?' This is a meaningless ordinance if there is no resurrection.

vv.30-32. 'For that matter, why do we expose ourselves to ridicule, suffering and even death if we entertain no hope of eternal life? If there is no resurrection, we would not only be of all men most miserable but also most stupid. I face death every day. If the dead rise not, what advantage do I have? If we have no hope of resurrection, let us live as the heathen live.'

v.33. '**Do not be deceived** by those who deny the resurrection and by such denial argue for a sinful course of life. If you listen to these people and are influenced by them, you will be corrupted, for evil companions, associations and communion have a bad influence on the lives and practices even of good men.'

v.34. '**Awake** from this condition of sleep and carelessness. **Awake to** truth, **righteousness** and godliness. Don't be deceived by the false teachers who deny the resurrection, for **there are some among you who have not a true knowledge of God**, the gospel of Christ and the hope of eternal life. **I say this to your shame.'**

The resurrection of the dead - III

1 Corinthians 15 : 35-44

v.35. There were some who denied the resurrection of the dead (v.12). The question is presented: 'How shall dead bodies be raised which have been in the earth so many years?' They have been reduced to dust, and this dust has undergone a thousand changes. With what bodies do they come out of their graves? Will they be the same bodies?

v. 36. Paul does not answer in anger nor call them fools in violation of Matthew 5:22, but he calls them foolish people who claim to be wise in the Scriptures and yet are ignorant of the power and ways of God (Gal. 3:1). He takes them to the farmer to learn the answer to these questions. When the farmer sows grain (whether wheat or corn), it must be put into the ground before it produces a stalk of fruit. The seed, being buried in the earth, corrupts, rots and dies; and in time it rises up as stalk, blade and full ear. This shows that the decaying of the body by death is not an objection to the resurrection, but really necessary to its resurrection. If God is able to quicken a grain of corn that is entirely dead and rotten, why should it be thought incredible that God should quicken dead bodies?

v. 37. The farmer does not take a full stalk of corn with full blade and ear and plant it in the earth; he only plants the bare grain. In other words, that which we plant is not the finished product but only bare grain. When a believer rises from the grave, it will be, in a sense, the same body but with infinite glories and excellencies, as the new stalk of corn is so much greater than the bare seed which was sown!

v. 38. God gives to the seed the kind of body which pleases him; yet none can deny that the body of corn or wheat which comes up is from the seed sown, though with a different body in respect to quality, beauty and usefulness. It is not the farmer, nor the sun, nor the rain, but God, by his power and sovereignty, who gives the seed a new and glorious body. So the resurrection of the dead is God's work. All the glory in which our bodies shall rise springs from his free grace and is bestowed on the same person who is buried in the grave.

v. 39. Paul is showing in these next verses that, though God will raise our bodies from the grave with flesh and bones, we shall rise with qualities and conditions much different from the flesh and bones which we now know. There is now a difference in flesh. All flesh, as we know it, is not the same. Humans, beasts, birds and fish are all flesh, yet not the same flesh.

vv. 40, 41. 'There are celestial bodies' (such as the sun, moon and stars) 'and terrestrial bodies' (men, beasts, birds and other elements). The celestial is greater than the terrestrial. Even in the celestial bodies, the sun has a greater glory than the moon, and the moon greater than the stars. He is not saying that there will be a difference in the risen bodies among themselves, but he is only stressing the great difference in what we shall be, compared to what we are now!

vv. 42-44. 'So is the resurrection of the dead.' The resurrection of the dead will be in real flesh, in our own flesh as to substance (the way we know it now), but as to its qualities, as different as human flesh from fish flesh! Our vile bodies shall be fashioned like unto Christ's glorious body (Phil. 3:21; 1 John 3:1, 2; Luke 24:36-43).

1. Our bodies are buried *in corruption,* sickness and disease and are subject to decay and putrefaction, but when we are raised from the dead, our new bodies will be immortal, no longer subject to disease, decay, nor corruption.

2. We are buried *in dishonour and shame.* We were conceived in sin, shapen in iniquity, brought forth from the womb speaking lies. Our whole existence from birth to death (in thought, word and deed) is sinful, shameful and dishonourable (Isa. 1:5, 6; Rom. 3:10-18). We shall be raised in glory — in perfect beauty and comeliness, physically and spiritually. There will be no cause for shame in any way (Gen. 2:25).

3. We are buried *in weakness.* We come into the world in great weakness. What is weaker than a new-born babe? When we become adults, we are weak before disease and injury. We are weak and frail and subject to thirst, hunger, weariness and finally death. We are weak before Satan, the world and our own passions (Gal. 5:17; Rom. 7:24). We shall be raised in power! We are raised by the power of God but with great power in ourselves. We shall no longer be subject to these enemies of the flesh, no longer dependent on food, nor subject to evil (which shall be no more). We shall know weariness no more; we shall know as we have been known (1 Cor. 13:12). We shall be raised in spiritual, physical and mental power.

4. We are buried a *natural* (physical) body. We shall be
raised a spiritual (supernatural) body. Now we have a body
generated from another body, supported by food, water,
breath and sleep. We are limited to time, places and information.
When we are raised, our bodies will be as the body of Christ is
now, not subject to nor dependent on these things. Our bodies
shall be beautiful, incorruptible, free from infirmities, not
subject to hunger, thirst or injuries, not needing meat, drink,
clothes, nor marriage, but bodies which perfectly obey – the
soul made perfect.

The resurrection of the dead - IV

1 Corinthians 15 : 45-58

In the preceding verse Paul says that our resurrected bodies
will be spiritual bodies. As we now bear the image of the first
man, Adam (from whom we descended), having a natural body
like his, so we shall one day bear the image of the second man,
the Lord Jesus, having a spiritual body like his!

v.45.   Adam was the first man made, the parent, head and
representative of all his posterity. Adam had a body which was
animated by the soul, which was supported by eating, drinking,
sleeping and which was capable of dying. The last Adam is the
Lord Jesus Christ, called Adam because he is really and truly
man. He was raised from the dead with a spiritual body – not
that it was changed into a spirit, for it still remained flesh and
bones (Luke 24:36-40); but it was no longer supported in an
animal way nor subject to the weaknesses of animal bodies.
It is called 'a quickening spirit' because it has life itself, and he
is called a quickening Spirit because he gives life (John 14:19).

vv.46, 47.   It is not the spiritual life which came first, but the
physical and then the spiritual. The first man was formed out

of the earth (Gen. 2:7), and the word there signifies red earth. He had an earthy constitution, like the earth out of which he was taken, and he was doomed to return to it. The second man is the Lord from heaven, in distinction from the first man, who was of the earth. Though he was formed in the womb of the virgin, was flesh of her flesh and was supported by earthly means, yet he was conceived by the Holy Spirit and is very God of very God.

vv.48, 49.   As was Adam's body, so are the bodies of those who descend from Adam. They are houses of clay which rise out of the earth, are maintained by the things of earth and will return to the earth. As in Christ's spiritual body after his resurrection (in which he now lives in heaven and in which he will come again), so will be the resurrected bodies of all believers (Acts 1:9-11; 1 John 3:2). As we have borne the image, frailty and mortality of our representative, Adam, having a body subject to sin, infirmity and death, so we shall one day bear the image of our representative, Christ Jesus, having a spiritual body created in righteousness and true holiness (Rom. 5:17-19).

v.50.   'Flesh and blood' here signifies our bodies in their present state. These cannot inherit the kingdom of God because they are corrupt, subject to disease, supported by corrupt things and dying. We must be changed; we must put on incorruption and immortality and be raised a spiritual body.

v.51.   Someone may say, 'But there will be many saints alive on earth in natural bodies, when Christ returns, who shall not die and be buried in the common way.' That is true, but they must be changed. Their natural bodies must be turned into spiritual bodies.

v.52.   This change will take place in a sudden moment. When the trumpet sounds, when Christ returns, when the dead are raised incorruptible, immortal and made like Christ, those who are alive shall also be changed (1 Thess. 4:16-18).

v.53.   God has decreed, and heaven requires, that our bodies be changed from their present state of mortality and corruption to immortality and incorruption before we can enter into eternal glory.

v.54.   This quotation is from Isaiah 25:8. Christ (by his obedience, death and resurrection) has obtained a full victory for all his elect over sin, the curse and condemnation of the law, death, the grave, judgement and hell. So when this glorious change takes place at his coming, this promise shall become a reality. He will swallow up all death in victory.

v.55.   The reference may be to a bee or a wasp which, having lost its sting, can do no more harm and is no longer feared. When believers arise from the grave, they shall fear the sting of death no more — it is gone. The grave gets its victory over all men, for we shall all lie there one day. But in that resurrection morning, when death is swallowed up in victory, we may reasonably ask, 'Now, grave, where is your boasted victory?'

v.56.   Death has a sting and it is sin, which is the cause of death (Rom. 5:12). If it were not for sin, death would have no power over us. Sin gives death power over us. The strength of sin is the law of God, without which there would be no sin. Sin is the transgression of the law. It is the law which binds sin upon us, pronounces us guilty and condemns us to death (Rom. 3:19; Gal. 3:10).

v.57.   'Thanks be unto God, who has given us the victory', over the law by answering in perfect obedience all of its demands, and over death and the grave by dying and rising again. He lives for evermore; and because we are one in him and with him by God's sovereign mercy and grace, we shall never die (Rom. 8:33-39).

v.58.   'Therefore, my beloved brethren, because we have such a blessed and certain hope of resurrection, victory over death and the grave and perfect conformity to the image of

Christ Jesus, let us **be steadfast and unmovable** in the doctrines of the gospel, in our walk with Christ, in the preaching of the gospel and in encouraging one another; for **your** faith, **labour** and hope are certainly **not in vain**.'

Collections, courage and comfort

1 Corinthians 16 : 1-24

This chapter concludes the epistle with some directions concerning a collection for the poor believers, with a word about his intentions to visit them again and with exhortations to watchfulness, courage and love.

v. 1. 'Now concerning offerings and collections of money which are to be given by believers for the support of ministers, for the preaching of the gospel here and in other lands, for the relief of the poor, for widows and for orphans: you are to do the same as I have instructed the churches of Galatia to do.' The Lord's people are generous, sharing with others what God has given to them (Acts 4:34, 35; 2 Cor. 8:7-9; 9:6, 7).

v. 2. It is plain from this and other scriptures that the early churches assembled on the first day of the week (John 20:19; Acts 20:7). When they assembled on this day, offerings were to be received.

1. The *persons* giving — everyone.

2. The *spirit* of the gift — willingly (2 Cor. 8:12; 9:7).

3. The *amount* given — to be based on what a man has and in proportion to his blessings (2 Cor. 8:12, 13). Paul did not want to take up any collections when he visited them lest people accuse him of covetousness.

vv. 3-7. 'When I arrive, I will send those whom you approve to Jerusalem to carry your gifts of love, and if it seems wise for me to go with them, I shall do so. I intend to pass through Macedonia, and it may be that I will spend the winter with you that you may provide the things necessary for my journey.'

The apostle is careful to base all of his journeys and his work on the will and providence of God. 'I will visit you, I will tarry with you, if the Lord permits' (James 4:13-15). We desire only that which is agreeable to the will of God.

vv. 8, 9.   Pentecost was the Feast of Harvest observed fifty days from the Passover. It is mentioned by the apostle, not as a feast that believers observed (for Christ fulfilled all those) but to point out the time he would stay in Ephesus. He desired to be in Jerusalem for Pentecost, not to keep it, but to preach the gospel to the many Jews from everywhere who would be there (Acts 20:16). 'I will remain this time in Ephesus, for God has opened to me here a great and effectual door.' By God's grace, Paul's ministry at Ephesus brought many to faith in Christ. 'I have many enemies here,' as there always are where the gospel is preached.

vv. 10, 11.   'If Timothy comes to Corinth (1 Cor. 4:17), see that you put him at ease, receive him well and care for him properly, for he is a minister of the gospel and engaged in the same work of the Lord that I am.' Paul always showed a deep love and concern for other preachers and a strong interest in their work. He told Philemon to receive Onesimus as he would receive Paul (Philem. 17).

v. 12.   Apollos was known to them and had preached among them (Acts 18:24-28). He is mentioned in 1 Corinthians 3:4-6, and some think he left because of the divisions. Paul wanted him to go back and preach at Corinth, but he did not feel led to go at this time. However, he would come when he had opportunity.

vv. 13, 14.   'Watch ye.' Be on guard against false doctrines and false teachers, set a watch on your hearts, tongues, actions and entire conduct, watch over one another to encourage,

edify and comfort. **'Stand fast in the faith,'** do not depart
from the grace of faith (Heb. 3:12; 10:38, 39) or from the
doctrine of faith (1 Cor. 15:1, 2). **'Quit you like men, be
strong,'** or behave like mature men, not like children whom
the least opposition will terrify and throw down, but be
courageous in the face of adversity. **'Let all things be done
with charity.'** Let all things be done in true love to God and
others, motivated by God's love for us (Eph. 4:32; 2 Cor. 5:14).

vv. 15, 16. 'Brethren, you know that Stephanas and his
household were the first converts in your country (1 Cor. 1:16)
and that they consecrated and devoted themselves to the
service of God's people. I exhort you to respect such leaders,
submit to them and follow their example, as well as everyone
else who co-operates with us and labours in the gospel' (Heb.
13:7, 17).

vv. 17, 18. It seems that the church had sent these men to
Ephesus to visit Paul, to acquaint him with the state of the
church and to encourage him. He said that their visit made up
for his absence from them and refreshed his spirit as well as
theirs. Such men are to be appreciated, acknowledged and
honoured.

v. 19. This verse carries greetings to the church at Corinth
from the churches in Asia and from Aquila and Priscilla and
the church which met in their house. Aquila was a Jew of
Pontus and Priscilla was his wife (Acts 18:2, 3).

v. 20. 'Salute one another with a sincere kiss of love and
friendship.' It is a holy kiss denoting true and pure motives
and thoughts (Rom. 16:16; 2 Cor. 13:12).

v. 21. Some think that Paul had someone write for him, but
to prevent counterfeits, and that the church might be assured
that this was from him, he wrote his salutation with his own
hand.

v. 22.   'If any man does not love our Lord Jesus Christ, he shall be *(anathema)* accursed. **Our Lord shall come!** *(Maranatha.)*

vv. 23, 24.   'The grace, favour and spiritual blessings of our Lord Jesus Christ be with you. I love you all in Christ and for Christ's sake!'

2 CORINTHIANS

Comforted to comfort

2 Corinthians 1 : 1-11

It is evident from the salutation that the apostle Paul is the author of this epistle and that it was written to the church at Corinth, probably from Philippi, a city of Macedonia, a year or so after the first epistle. In this epistle Paul defends his office and gospel against false teachers, urges the church to comfort and restore the fallen brother, writes of the true glory of God and reconciliation to God which is only seen in and accomplished by Christ Jesus, tells of his sufferings and afflictions in the service of Christ and gives perhaps the fullest instructions concerning collections, offerings and giving to be found anywhere in the New Testament.

v.1. Paul identifies himself by name and office. His salutation is much the same as is found in other epistles and reveals that the true servants of Christ are not fond of fancy titles, before or after their names, and they ascribe their offices and authority to the will and call of God. God put Paul in the ministry and gave him his gifts (1 Tim. 1:12-14). In humility (characteristic of Paul) he includes young Timothy in this greeting, calling him **'our brother'** in the grace of God and the ministry of the gospel. The epistle is addressed to the church at Corinth and to all believers in that region.

v.2. **'Grace be to you and peace from God our Father, and from the Lord Jesus Christ.'** Paul prays for an increase of grace, for every grace is imperfect in us, and those who have the most stand in need of more (2 Peter 3:18; 1 Peter 1:1-3). By **'peace'** is meant peace with God through Christ, peace and contentment in our own hearts and peace among believers and with all men. The Father is the giver and Christ is the fountain of all grace and peace in this life and throughout eternity.

v.3.   The word **'blessed'** means to praise, to thank, to speak
of in the highest adoration and to give all glory to our eternal
God. He is described as **'the Father of our Lord Jesus Christ,'**
not by creation, as angels and men, nor by adoption as believers,
but by eternal generation, having the same nature with him
and equal to him in perfection, power and glory (John 1:1-3).
The title 'Father' denotes his covenant relation to the Mediator
and his seed (Gal. 3:16). He is called **'the Father of mercies'**
even as life, love, light and all mercies are from God (Micah
7:18), physical, material and spiritual! And he is called **'the
God of all comfort'**. There is no comfort nor rest except from
him and in him. Whatever comfort believers enjoy, they have
from the Father, who is their covenant God, through Christ,
who is their Redeemer and Mediator and by the Holy Spirit,
who is called the Comforter.

v.4.   Two things are evident from this verse.
     1. The apostle attributed all comfort, strength and grace,
which he experienced in trials and tribulations, to God (Heb.
13:5, 6) as the fountain of mercies.
     2. The gifts, grace and comforts which God bestows upon
us are not merely for our own use, but in order that we may
help and comfort others by the comfort we have from our
Lord.

v.5.   **'The sufferings of Christ'** are not those which he suffered
himself in our stead, but the persecution, afflictions and trials
which ministers and believers endure on earth because of the
gospel and opposition from men (2 Cor. 4:7-10). Christ called
Saul's persecution of believers a persecuting of himself (Acts
9:4; Matt. 25:40). God multiplies his comfort in Christ according to the measure of his trials. As our afflictions increase, so
do our comforts in order that we may comfort others and not
be overwhelmed with grief.

v.6.   The afflictions and comfort, the sufferings and blessings

of the apostles and other ministers of the gospel were all for
the good of believers, who saw their boldness, submission and
courage in trial, heard their comforting words (Phil. 1 :13, 14)
and were encouraged to endure with faith the same trials. The
spirit and attitude we exhibit both in trial and comfort have a
great and lasting effect upon those to whom we minister the
Word (Phil. 4:11-13; 2 Cor. 4:15-18). God uses men as ambassadors and examples (1 Cor. 10:11; 1 Peter 5:3).

v. 7.   **'Our hope for you'** – that is, 'our confident expectation
of the good work of God in regeneration, sanctification and
justification in Christ, which is begun in your souls, will be
carried on and perfected. You will continue in the faith and
not be moved away from your profession of Christ by the
afflictions and trials which you see in us and experience
yourselves. Just as you share and are partners in our sufferings,
you share and are partners in our comfort.'

vv. 8, 9.   We are not sure about the troubles Paul refers to in
this verse but, whatever they were, he says they were so great
that he despaired even of life, for these trials were above his
natural strength to bear them. It was his opinion that he would
die, but God brought him to this extreme condition that he
might lay aside all trust and confidence in human strength,
wisdom and power to survive and be encouraged to trust in
God alone, who raised the dead. If he is able to raise the dead,
so he is able to deliver us at all times. Abraham believed this
(Heb. 11 :17-19).

v. 10.   The Lord in mercy delivered us from this heavy
affliction and, knowing that we are continually exposed to
danger and death, he will continue to preserve and protect us!
All three tenses – past, present and future – are mentioned,
which shows Paul's confidence in God's goodness in delivering
us out of troubles for his glory and our good. This confidence
can also apply to our redemption. We have been saved (Eph.
2:8, 9), we are being saved (1 Cor. 1:18), and our salvation is
nearer than when we believed (Rom. 13:11).

v.11.   Faith in God's purpose, power and sovereignty ought not to discourage prayer, the use of means, nor intercession for one another (James 4:2; Matt. 7:7, 8). 'You prayed for us and God was pleased to deliver us. Therefore, for this gift bestowed upon us by the means of many praying, many ought also to give thanks to God on our behalf.' We ought to pray for those in distress, but we ought also to give thanks when prayers are heard.

All God's promises in Christ are yes

2 Corinthians 1 : 12-24

In the First Epistle to the Corinthians (1 Cor. 16:1-7) Paul indicated that he would stop in Corinth on his way to Macedonia and, after he had finished his business in Macedonia, he would come back to Corinth and spend a long time with them. Although these were his plans, the Lord ordered otherwise and Paul did not visit them. This change of plans caused many problems. Some accused Paul of levity, unfaithfulness, going back on his word and several other things. The enemies of Paul and the false teachers tried to capitalize on this and destroy Paul's influence with the Corinthian church.

v.12.   Paul answers the charge that he had falsified his word in not coming to Corinth as he had promised, by appealing to his own conscience, integrity in the faith and sincerity towards the glory of God and his church. 'I rejoice to inform you and all others that my conscience and conduct, my heart and mouth behave together **in simplicity** (not double-mindedness) **and godly sincerity** (as opposed to hypocrisy); **not with fleshly wisdom** (craftiness to accomplish selfish ends) **but by the grace of God** dwelling in me, I have acted in the world and especially towards you in sincerity and truth.'

v.13. 'There is no double meaning to what we say or write. The things which I write are what you know and must acknowledge to be truth (1 Thess. 2:13; 2 Peter 1:20,21). I hope you will acknowledge them to be true to the end of your lives.'

v.14. **'In part'** may refer to persons or things. 'A part of you have owned us to be sincere ministers of God and have rejoiced and blessed God that you heard us, though others of you have abused us.' Or, 'You have in part (at one time) owned us and had cause to thank God for us. When the Lord Jesus shall come to judge the world in righteousness, I shall rejoice that my labour among you has not been in vain.' What a blessing when ministers and people rejoice in each other here, and their joy shall be complete in that day!

vv.15, 16. 'Therefore, being persuaded of your affection for me and my rejoicing in you and your love for Christ, I fully intended and promised to come to visit you on the way to Macedonia. The benefit you received from my first visit was to hear the gospel and be converted to Christ, so a **second benefit** would be your edification and growth in grace! I planned to visit you on the way to Macedonia and on my return, and to have you help me on my way to Judea.' Yet, for some reason, Paul changed his plans. He deals with the matter further in verse 23 and chapter 2:1-3.

v.17. 'When I originally planned to come to you and put it in writing, did I do it lightly and carelessly, with no regard to God's will and your good? Did I not say, "If the Lord permit"? (1 Cor. 16:6,7.) Do I purpose according to the flesh? Do I consult my own interest and advantage? Do I say, "Yes," when I may mean, "No"? Do my lips say one thing and my heart another?'

vv.18, 19. The false teachers and enemies of grace had suggested that since Paul had not kept his word in coming to them as he promised, then he was not to be depended upon in his ministry. Paul declares that as God was true to his promises,

so he had taught Paul to be true to his words to them. He calls
the Lord to be his witness that his words preached among
them and his personal words to them were true, honest and
sincere — not 'yes' and 'no'. 'Our intentions and plans are
subject to the will and providence of the Lord; his promises in
Christ are not subject to change (Mal. 3:6; Rom. 11:29). For
the eternal Son of God, Jesus Christ our Surety, Redeemer,
Mediator, Prophet, Priest and King, whom we preached to you
and in whom we have life through his person and work, is not
"yes" and "no", but all of God's promises in him are "yes"!'

v.20.   God has made many promises to believers. These
promises are all in Christ, since only he existed when they
were made and since he has fulfilled all conditions by his
obedience and death. Therefore, these promises are all 'yes'
and in him 'amen' or 'so be it'. 'Christ fulfilling, our preaching
and your believing are all for the glory of God' (Eph. 1:6, 12).

vv.21, 22.   Now it is God who chose us in Christ, redeemed
us in Christ, called us in Christ and secures us for ever together
in Christ. It is God who anoints us with his Spirit and presence
in regeneration and in ministerial gifts. It is God who has
owned us as his own, putting his seal upon us (Phil. 1:6). It is
God who has given us the Holy Spirit himself as an earnest or
pledge of the heavenly inheritance (2 Cor. 5:5; Eph. 1:13, 14).

v.23.   Paul gives a hint as to the reason why he did not come
to visit them. 'I call upon God as my soul's witness; it was to
avoid hurting you that I refrained from coming to Corinth.
With all the disorders among you, I would have had to come
with the rod of correction. I am hoping for a reformation
among you that when I do come, it may be with joy.'

v.24.   'Not that I have dominion over you or your faith;
Christ is the author and object of faith.' The minister can
neither give faith nor sustain it. We are but helpers, or means
and instruments, which God uses to preach the gospel and to
instruct believers (1 John 1:3, 4; 1 Cor. 3:5-9).

Who is sufficient for these things?

2 Corinthians 2 : 1-17

In the early verses of this chapter the apostle gives a reason
why he did not come to Corinth as was expected. He was
unwilling to grieve them or be grieved by them. He preferred
to have a cheerful visit to them, and this would have been
impossible with the divisions, disorders and unjudged sin
among them. He desired to have his instructions, which were
given in the first epistle, carried out so that his next visit might
be to teach and not to bear the rod.

vv. 1, 2.   Paul made up his mind that he would not go to
Corinth in sorrow and heaviness, rebuking and censuring them
for their disorders. He had already done this in the previous
epistle, which was a sort of coming to them and by which he
made them sorry. If his visit was to be one of rebuke and
conflict, which would be the means of fresh grief and sorrow,
what pleasure and joy would he have among them?

v. 3.   This was the purpose of his first epistle, that when he
came again to Corinth, he might not be pained by those who
ought to make him rejoice. He had written in confidence that
they would correct the things that were amiss among them.

v. 4.   Paul preached in Corinth eighteen months. After he left
Corinth, false teachers crept in and disturbed the church with
false doctrine and unscriptural practices. The church fell into
divisions, factions and misuse of gifts, questions arose about
marriage and going to law with one another, members were
allowed to live in open sin without being disciplined, the
resurrection was questioned, ordinances were abused and they
flaunted their learning and gifts. Paul wrote the first epistle to

them out of much sorrow, distress and tears, not just to cause them grief but that they might realize the great love he had for them. True ministers and other believers who reprove and rebuke error of doctrine, spirit and conduct show their love for us and their concern for our spiritual welfare.

vv. 5-8. In these verses Paul deals with the matter of the man who was guilty of incest (1 Cor. 5:1, 2). The man, evidently a preacher, teacher, or gifted man, was living in open sin with his stepmother. Equally shocking to Paul was the fact that the church held the man in esteem and overlooked his conduct. Paul instructed them to discipline him strongly (1 Cor. 5:3-5), which they evidently did, for he now instructs them to comfort, forgive and receive him back into their fellowship. 'The man's behaviour has not only grieved me but in some measure all of you.' Now the public rebuke and excommunication by so many was sufficient punishment. The man was broken, humbled and truly repentant. Therefore, they ought now to forgive him, comfort him and reinstate him to keep him from being overwhelmed by excessive sorrow and despair (Gal. 6:1). Paul exhorts them to reinstate him and to express their love to him in the most kind and tender manner.

v. 9. This was my purpose in writing you then and my purpose in writing now that I might prove your faith, love and obedience to Christ, his Word, and his apostles in all things! When the apostles write these epistles under the power of God's Spirit, God speaks! (Luke 10:16; 1 John 4:6; 2 Tim. 3:16.)

vv. 10, 11. 'Remember that when you forgive and comfort this man or any other, I forgive them, too. I readily forgive for Christ's sake, in the name of Christ, and in conformity to his teaching and example (Eph. 4:32; Mark 11:25, 26). I also forgive for your sake or for the good and advantage of the church, before the presence of Christ! I am aware of Satan's ways and devices.' He will use any means against the Lord and his church. If he can foster division, an unforgiving spirit, harsh feelings, or pride in the church, he will do it. He will, under pretence of showing indignation against sin, keep a strict and harsh attitude towards offenders, destroy souls and convince men that they are serving God in their self-righteous attitudes (2 Cor. 11:13-15).

vv.12, 13. When Paul journeyed to Troas (Acts 20:6) to preach the gospel of Christ, God was pleased to open the door for him. This indicates the liberty he had to preach, the hearing he received, or a measure of success which God gave to his ministry (1 Cor. 16:9). Paul was grieved that his brother (in the faith), Titus, was not there to give him an account of the church at Corinth (2 Cor. 7:5-7). He journeyed on to Macedonia, where Titus met him and refreshed his spirit with a good report from Corinth.

v.14. 'Blessed be God and thanks be unto God, who, though we have many enemies, yet through Christ makes us more than conquerors and accomplishes his purpose through us. In every place we preach God reveals the sweet fragrance of Christ. As when a box of priceless perfume is opened, the fragrance fills the place and everyone smells it or is aware of it.

vv.15, 16. To those whose hearts are opened by the Spirit of God, who feel the guilt of sin and who see the beauty of Christ, the substitute and sin offering, this gospel is the sweet fragrance of life unto life – spiritual life now and life everlasting. But to those who are perishing, whose hearts are hardened and who are filled with pride and unbelief, this fragrance of Christ is an offensive odour. Their rejection of our gospel only adds to their condemnation. Eternal death is added to spiritual death; death *for* sin is added to death *in* sin. **'Who is sufficient for these things?'** What man is sufficient for such a mighty work, such responsibility, such an awesome task? Who is worthy to speak for God? No one! But our sufficiency is Christ (2 Cor. 3:5).

v.17. Paul declares that he does not, like so many hucksters, false preachers and flesh merchants, make merchandise of and deal deceitfully with the Word of God. But in sincerity and with the purest motive (for the glory of God and the eternal salvation of men), he preaches Christ and him crucified in the presence of God and by the power of God!

Ministers of the new covenant

2 Corinthians 3 : 1-6

In the preceding verses the apostle Paul spoke very plainly in defence of his ministry, having stated that God always caused him and his fellow ministers to triumph in Christ, that they were a sweet fragrance of Christ unto God and to their hearers and that they did not corrupt the Word of God (as some did) but preached faithfully the gospel of God's grace and mercy in Christ.

v.1. 'Are we bragging about ourselves? Are we guilty of vain glory? Are we seeking to commend ourselves, or are we recommending ourselves to you and seeking letters of recommendation from you to others? Some preachers may feel the need of credentials and letters of recommendation from place to place, but we do not need them.'

v.2. 'You are our credentials; you are our letters of recommendation.' Paul was God's messenger to them and the instrument God used to bring them to a knowledge of Christ (Rom. 10:13-15; 2 Cor. 5:20, 21). Their embracing the gospel of Christ, their faith, holiness and love and their perseverance in grace were testimonials to all men that God was with Paul and that God had sent him. They were written in his heart, not statistics and glowing reports on paper!

v.3. He told them in the previous verse that they were his epistles written on his heart and did more to recommend him than all the reports on paper. But he is careful to ascribe to the Lord Jesus all the glory, for he says here that they are really the epistles of Christ! Paul is only the instrument the Lord used to preach to them. It was Christ, who, by his Spirit, wrote his law on their hearts, shed abroad his love in their hearts and saved them by his grace (Rom. 5:5-9; Eph. 2:8-10). The law of Christ is written not on tables of stone, as at Sinai, but on the heart of the believer (Ezek. 36:26, 27; Jer. 31:33).

v.4. 'This is the hope, trust and confidence that we have through Christ toward, and with reverence to God. God has saved and called us to preach, through our ministry has called you to faith and has given us all access to his throne of grace through the person and work of Christ, our Lord. This is our hope and confidence (Col. 1:12-23; 2:9, 10).

v.5. Although Paul strongly defended his call to preach and declared that the Corinthians were proof and the fruits of his ministry, he would not leave the impression that he ascribed anything to himself, to any power or sufficiency in himself. He says that we are not sufficient even to think (which is the lowest human act) anything truly and spiritually good, much less sufficient for so great a work as the conversion of a soul. 'Our power, ability and sufficiency are of God. His grace is sufficient to enable us to repent, believe, embrace Christ and preach, and to enable you to receive our gospel (2 Cor. 5:18, 19). God did not find us sufficient, but he made us sufficient. The best preacher of the gospel is no more than what the grace of God makes him (1 Cor. 15:10).

v.6. '**God has made us,** or qualified us, to be **ministers of the new covenant,** or the covenant of grace, of which Jesus Christ is the Mediator and Surety.' In the following verses the apostle makes a comparison between the old covenant and the new, the law of Moses and the free grace and gospel of Christ (Heb. 8:6; 12:24; 13:20). The covenant of grace is called 'the

new covenant', not because it is newly made (for it is the
everlasting covenant) nor even because it is newly revealed (for
it is revealed in prophecy, promise and types throughout the
Old Testament) but because it is now fulfilled in the person
and work of Christ, it is now manifested clearly in the gospel
message (Rom. 3:21, 22), and it is forever new; it will never
give way to another covenant (Heb. 10:9, 10). 'We are ministers,
not of the letter of the law' (Rom. 7:6), which shows what is
to be done, thought and said and what is not to be done,
without giving any ability to obey its commands and with no
power to sanctify or justify those who are under it (Rom.
3:19, 20), 'but we are ministers of the gospel which, in the
hands of the Holy Spirit, gives spiritual life and eternal life.'
The bare letter of the law kills, in that it reveals sin, inability
and enmity (Rom. 7:7-10; Gal. 3:10). The gospel of Christ is
the Spirit who gives life, quickening dead sinners, working
true repentance toward God and faith in Christ, writing the
commandments of God on the heart and mind, and who
actually justifies, sanctifies and makes the believer a new
creature in Christ (2 Cor. 5:17; Gal. 5:22). We must be careful
not to minister the gospel in letter and doctrine only, but in
demonstration of the Spirit and power (1 Cor. 2:1-5).

The veil removed by Christ

2 Corinthians 3 : 7-18

In verse 6 the apostle observed the difference between the old
covenant and the new, and the excellency of the gospel over
the law. The law is a killing letter; the gospel is a quickening
Spirit. In the following verses he reveals other ways in which
they differ and further shows the glory of the gospel of Christ
above the law of Moses.

vv. 7-9.   1. The Old Testament dispensation was **'the ministration of death'**. It discovered and revealed sin; it showed the wrath and curse of God; it showed man his duty, but gave no strength to perform it. The New Testament is the ministration of the *Spirit and life* in the gospel of Christ, which reveals Christ as our righteousness and which reveals the grace and mercy of God through Christ unto life everlasting. The law shows God above us and against us; the gospel reveals Emmanuel, 'God with us.'

2. The law was written and **'engraved on tables of stone'**, whereas the gospel is *written on the heart* (Heb. 10:15, 16).

3. The law and the giving of the law were **'glorious'** (Exod. 20:18-21; 34:29, 30). Much of the glory and majesty of God attended the giving of the law — the glory of his presence, justice and holiness. But the gospel reveals the *greater glory of God* — the glory of his grace and mercy and the glory of his beloved Son in substitution and satisfaction for guilty sinners (Exod. 33:18,19). This gospel is ministered by his Holy Spirit.

4. The law is **'the ministration of condemnation'** only, for it cannot forgive, cleanse, nor offer any hope. Now if this be glorious, think how glorious is the gospel of Christ, which provides a perfect righteousness and right standing before God and produces love and obedience to God (Gal. 3:13, 14; 2 Cor. 5:21; 1 Cor. 1:30).

v.10.   In view of this fact, the glory of the law and the glory shown in the face of Moses have come to have no glory and splendour at all because of the overwhelming glory of the gospel of God revealed in our Lord Jesus Christ (2 Cor. 4:5, 6).

v.11.   If the law of Moses (fulfilled in and by Christ), which was but temporary and has been done away, was glorious, how much more glorious is the covenant of grace and righteousness in Christ, which abides for ever! (Heb. 10:9-14.)

v.12.   The word **'hope'** here is more than a wish or a good prospect. It is a confident expectation based on the sure Word of God and the person and work of Christ. The meaning of the verse is 'Since we have a certain and confident expectation of acceptance by God in Christ, of everlasting righteousness and of eternal glory which can never pass away, we are neither ashamed nor afraid to preach this gospel to all men.'

v. 13. We preach the gospel of the glory of God (1 Tim. 1:11) freely, openly and boldly and not like Moses, who put a veil over his face, not so the people could not look, but because they could not bear to look upon even the reflected glory of God (Exod. 34:30-35). And because of their unbelief and hardness of heart, they could not see the end or goal of that law, who is Christ (Rom. 10:1-4).

vv. 14, 15. Moses' covering of his face with a veil signifies the righteousness of God in Christ, which is hid from generations because of unbelief and hardness of heart (Col. 1:26, 27; Rom. 11:7, 8). To this day that same veil remains, and they do not see the glory of the gospel nor Christ, the end of the law. They read the Old Testament Scriptures but cannot see Jesus Christ in them (Acts 10:43; Luke 24:27, 44-46). This veil can only be removed through the light of the gospel of Christ shining in the heart. When a person sees Christ by faith, he sees the unveiled glory of God (John 14:9).

v. 16. Nevertheless, when a person (Jew or Gentile, one person or a nation such as Israel) shall turn from unbelief, idolatry and salvation by the works of the law to the Lord Jesus Christ in true repentance and faith, that veil of blindness shall be removed. Some understand this of the whole of the Jews in a future day (Rom. 11:25, 26), and it may be, but all men are spiritually blind who have not seen the glory of God in Christ. When we see the Son in his redemptive power and work, we see the fulfilment of the law, satisfaction of God's justice and the glory of God!

v. 17. The Lord to whom we turn when the veil is taken away is the Lord Jesus Christ. He is the man Christ Jesus, but not only a mere man; he is that Spirit or he is God (John 4:24).

He is the Spirit of grace, peace and life. He is the giver and the
gift of the Spirit, and where he lives and dwells, there is liberty
— emancipation from the bondage of the law, the curse of the
law and the penalty of the law. 'If the Son shall make you free,
you shall be free indeed.'

v.18.   The Israelites saw the glory of God in a cloud, in the
tabernacle and in the types and shadows, but all believers with
unveiled and open faces behold the glory of God with eyes of
faith in the face of Christ Jesus. Not that we look upon the
full majestic glory of God himself, for no man could do this
and live (Exod. 33:20). But we behold his glory as in a mirror
(1 Cor. 13:12), and by looking to him in faith, we grow in
grace and the knowledge of Christ. From one degree of grace
and faith to another, we are changed, and the image of Christ
is formed in the believer. This comes by the Spirit and power
of God.

The face of Jesus Christ

2 Corinthians 4 : 1-6

Because of much persecution, suffering and affliction, Paul
had to battle against the accusations by false teachers that he
was not a true apostle of Christ. These men tried to prejudice
the minds of the people against Paul and his friends. In this
chapter he declares his uncompromising zeal and integrity in
preaching the gospel, so that if any did not see the glory and
truth of it, it was because they were blinded by Satan and the
hardness of their own hearts, not from want of a true minister
and a true message.

v.1.   'Therefore, seeing we have this ministry of the Spirit
and life (written on the heart, not in letter but spirit) of
justification and a perfect righteousness through Christ, this

ministry of the redemptive glory of God in the person and
work of Christ, we do not get discouraged nor faint in our
spirit because of difficulties and trials (John 16:33; 2 Tim.
3:12; Phil. 1:29). Our call to the ministry is by the mercy and
grace of God, as is our strength and power to persevere through
many hardships' (2 Cor. 12:9; Acts 18:9, 10). The best man
would faint under the work and perish under trial and burdens
without the mercy and grace of God (1 Cor. 15:10).

v.2.   'We renounce **the hidden things of dishonesty'** — that is,
they were the same men in private as they were in public. In
regard to conduct, conversation and doctrine, they were open
and above board (Matt. 7:15). The false teachers have much to
hide in motive, manners and methods; they speak one thing in
secret and another in the congregation. 'We do not **walk in
craftiness**, practising trickery and cunning, using people to
further our gain and glory, disguising our true goals.' There are
many hucksters and merchandisers of souls who use religion
and the gospel to promote themselves and not the glory of
God (2 Peter 2:1-3). 'We do not **handle the Word of God
deceitfully**,' corrupting it with human work, tradition and
philosophy. 'We do not keep back a part of it, twist it to suit
the flesh, and cry "peace" when there is no peace (Gal. 2:21;
Acts 20:20, 27). We **commend ourselves** (in the presence and
sight of God) **to every man's conscience** by preaching with
plainness and boldness the truth of the gospel as it is revealed
in the Lord Jesus' (Heb. 13:17). An upright way of life and a
true message of Christ crucified are all the recommendations a
minister needs before men and women who know God.

v.3.   The apostle calls the gospel **'our gospel'** because he was
saved by it, he was an instrument of God called to preach it,
he was in love with and obsessed by it and he was entrusted
with it (1 Tim. 1:11, 12). If that blessed gospel of the grace of
God be hidden so that men do not understand, receive and
believe it, the fault is not in the gospel nor in the preaching of
it, but in the men themselves. For they are lost, blind, dead,
natural men who have no spiritual perception nor taste for the

things of God (1 Cor. 2:14,15). All mankind are in a lost condition by birth and because of sin. God has purposed to save the lost through Christ (Luke 19:10). He chose some, Christ redeemed them and the Spirit calls them by the gospel. However, many will be lost for ever, left in blindness and sin under the dominion of Satan. Some writers believe these who will be lost for ever are the people referred to in verses 3 and 4.

v.4. 'The god of this world' (because of the context and the work of deception and blinding man's eyes to the gospel) can only refer to Satan. Nowhere else do we find him called by this name, but our Lord twice referred to him as 'the prince of this world' (John 12:31; 14:30). What he blinds is 'the mind' — the understanding. Those who believe not are under the influence of Satan (Eph. 2:1-3), who penetrates hearts and minds with prejudice, pride, error and ignorance. By divine permission, he bears great power in the world and in the hearts of men. His design is to keep men in darkness and ignorance and, while he cannot keep the gospel out of this world, his business is to keep it out of men's hearts. The glorious gospel is the gospel of God's glory (Exod. 33:18, 19) in Christ. Christ, who is the express image and revelation of God, is the sum and substance of the gospel (Rom. 1:1-3) and salvation is having Christ revealed to and in us (Gal. 1:15).

v.5. 'We preach not ourselves, our opinions, our philosophies, nor do we preach to promote ourselves nor supply ourselves with life's necessities. We preach **Christ Jesus, the Lord** (1 Cor. 2:2). We preach *Christ,* the Messiah, Prophet, Priest and King, fulfilment of every Old Testament type and promise; *Jesus,* Son of man, Man of sorrows, numbered with the transgressors, tempted in all points; the *Lord,* very God of very god, King of kings and Lord of lords. We are your servants for his sake' (Matt. 20:26, 27).

v.6. In the creation of the world, God made something out of nothing. He commanded light to shine in darkness (Gen. 1:3). So in the new creation in Christ, God makes something

out of nothing and commands the light (Christ is the light) to
shine into our darkened hearts to give us the true knowledge
of God and his glory (1 John 5:20). As light was the first
production in creation, so the light of Christ is the first thing
in the new creation. Conviction of sin (John 16:8-10), the
honouring of the law (Rom. 5:19), the satisfaction of God's
justice (Rom. 3:25,26), and faith (Gal. 2:20) are all accomplished in the sinner in relation to Christ Jesus. Even our
spiritual growth is in the grace and knowledge of Christ
(2 Peter 3:18). So from the new birth to perfect conformity to
Christ, the whole of the work of redemption is relative to
Christ.

Cast down but not destroyed

2 Corinthians 4 : 7-18

v. 7.   The gospel of Christ is called a **'treasure'** in that it
contains rich truth; it has rich blessings, such as redemption,
sanctification and justification; it consists of rich and precious
promises; it shows forth the riches of God's grace and mercy in
Christ. This treasure is **'in earthen vessels'**, meaning the ministers
to whom God entrusts the gospel and through whom he sends
the gospel to sinners. They are weak and frail creatures, subject
to like passions and infirmities as other men (James 5:17;
1 Cor. 2:5-7). God makes the most unlikely his instruments of
grace, that he might have all the glory (1 Cor. 1:26-29). The
weaker the vessel, the stronger his power appears to be.
Whatever is accomplished in the proclamation of the gospel by
frail men is the work of God and not men, that he, not they,
might be praised and glorified.

vv. 8, 9.   **'We are troubled'** and oppressed in every way. We are
never free from one trial or another. We are in the world and
expect tribulations (John 16:1-4, 33; 15:19, 20), yet we are

'**not distressed**'. We have the peace of God, the manifestations of his love and care, a freedom to the throne and sufficient grace for every trial (2 Cor. 12:9). '**We are perplexed**'; the word signifies doubting and uncertainty. We are often uncertain and in doubt about what will happen to us; and sometimes we know not what to do, which way to take, nor how our needs shall be supplied, but we are '**not in despair**'. We do not despair of the leadership, help, presence and support of our Lord. We are '**persecuted**' of men, cursed, threatened and despised because we profess Christ and preach Christ crucified, risen and exalted. But we are '**not forsaken**' of our Lord, who owns us and causes us always to triumph in Christ (2 Cor. 2:14). Neither are we forsaken by those who love Christ, for they support us in prayer and provisions. We are '**cast down**' like an earthen vessel is sometimes cast out or thrown to the earth, seemingly forgotten and deserted. But we are '**not destroyed**'. We live by the mighty power of God and are immortal until his work in us, through us and by us is done. Whatever the condition of God's children in this world, they have a 'but not' to comfort them. Their case may be bad, but not hopeless; for he is their hope!

vv. 10, 11.   Paul speaks here of the sufferings and afflictions the disciples themselves endure in the flesh. We are liable to the same hatred, suffering and putting to death that our Lord suffered. We are one with him, and the world, which hates him, hates us. We don't expect any better treatment than was afforded our Lord. There is one great consolation: 'Because he lives, we shall live.' The power of our Lord's grace, strength, comfort and peace is in us daily, manifested to us, to the church and to the world. The apostles and ministers of the gospel seem to be a special target for Satan's hatred and the world's enmity, but even these trials God uses to call out his sheep (2 Tim. 2:9, 10) through their word.

v. 12.   'Our death is your life; our sufferings are for your advantage. This gospel we preach at the expense of persecution, trial and even death is the means of bringing the gospel of life to you.'

v.13. Paul declares that he and his fellow labourers have the same spirit of faith as David, who wrote in Psalm 116:10, 'I believed, and therefore have I spoken.' We, too, believe God, his eternal purpose in Christ, man's utter ruin and inability, the person and work of our Lord Jesus, the resurrection to eternal life of believers and the resurrection to eternal condemnation of unbelievers. Therefore we speak these truths. The Old Testament saints are our examples (Rom. 4:19-25).

v.14. We are assured that God, who raised our Lord Jesus from the grave as the first-fruits of them who sleep, shall by the same power flowing from him who sits at his right hand also raise our mortal bodies from the grave. We know that Christ was raised and his resurrection is an assurance of ours (1 Cor. 15:20-27). We shall all meet in the resurrection (1 Thess. 4:13-18) and shall, by Christ, be presented unto God, redeemed by his life and washed in his blood (Jude 24, 25).

v.15. **'All these things'** that the apostle has mentioned (from the eternal purpose of God in electing a people, the prophecies, promises and types of the Old Testament, the incarnation, obedience, death, resurrection and exaltation of our Lord, to the calling, preaching and sufferings of the apostles) **'are for your sakes!'** The more the grace, favour and blessings of God are revealed to multitudes, the more honour, glory and praise are given to our God (1 Cor. 1:30, 31).

v.16. 'Therefore, we ministers of the gospel do not become discouraged, nor do we have thoughts of quitting the conflict. Our outward flesh is progressively decaying and wasting away, but our inward man, created in Christ Jesus, everyday grows stronger and stronger in the grace and faith of Christ.'

v.17. Paul calls our sufferings in the flesh for the sake of Christ **'light afflictions'**. That which the flesh calls heavy, burdensome and grievous, faith perceives to be light and but for the moment. When we are being used of God, supported by his grace, favoured with his love, and know that these trials are for our good and his glory, we are able to call them 'light afflictions'. Then when we compare these afflictions and time on earth with the glory that shall be ours, they become even less important (Rom. 8:18).

v.18. Someone once said that two things support the believer who is under trial: firstly, seeing the Lord's purpose and hand in it all (Heb. 11:27; Rom. 8:28) and secondly, looking by faith beyond this world to that glory which God had prepared for those who love him (Heb. 11:9, 10). The things of this world that we see, feel and taste by faith through the grace of God are eternal.

Absent from the body - present with the Lord

2 Corinthians 5 : 1-10

This chapter continues the subject dealt with in the closing verses of chapter 4. Two things support the believer under trial and suffering: seeing him who is invisible and seeing the glory which is to follow this brief life on earth. Our confident hope of an eternal, blessed life with Christ hereafter makes us indifferent to our temporary troubles and encourages us to seek only our Lord's approval.

v.1. These are things which **'we know'**. The body in which the soul dwells is an **'earthly house'** because it is from the earth (Gen. 3:19) and shall return to the earth. It is called a **'tabernacle'** or tent because of its frailty and short existence. It must soon wear out, be folded together and finally destroyed (Heb. 9:27). When this comes to pass and the body is laid in the ground, the spirit returns to God (Luke 23:43; Phil. 1:23). We have **'in the heavens'** a house, or habitation, or dwelling-place made by God, through the righteousness and death of Christ (John 14:1-3). It is a 'building of God' (worthy of its Author), 'eternal' (in that it shall never perish), and it will be enjoyed immediately after this tent is dissolved.

v.2. Two things are evident here.

1. The believer groans under the burdens of this life. He groans because of the nature and corruption of sin which remains in him (Rom. 7:24, 25).

2. The believer longs and desires to be free from all sin and to be like Christ (Ps. 17:15). He does not desire death just for the sake of being done with life's burdens and trials, but he desires to put on immortality and to enter into the eternal joys of his Lord.

v.3. We shall enter into the presence of the Lord clothed in the shining, pure and perfect robes of Christ's righteousness and shall not be ashamed (nor cast out) being naked (Matt. 22:11-13).

v.4. While we are still in this tent of flesh, 'we do groan, being burdened' with the body of flesh and sin and desiring to be with Christ, which is far better. It is not that we desire to cease to exist nor cease to live in God's universe and kingdom, but that we long to live truly in glory, holiness and immortality (1 Cor. 15:51-54). There is death about us and in us, and we long to be done with it. Death is not to be desired for its own sake, but even in the flesh we rejoice in the Lord and in his good providence. But death is to be desired because it leads the believer to that glorious change into the image of Christ.

v.5. It is our sovereign Lord who has chosen, redeemed and called us to that glory and immortality (Rom. 8:28-31). We can be sure of that inheritance, for God, in his unchangeable purpose (Mal. 3:6), has determined to populate the new heaven and new earth with a people like Christ. He gave his Son to redeem them and to provide for them a perfect righteousness, and he has given us his Holy Spirit as a pledge of that promise (Eph. 1:13, 14). Salvation is of the Lord in its plan, its execution, its application, its continuation and its ultimate perfection.

v.6. Because God has foreordained us unto eternal glory in, by and through Christ, and has given us the earnest of his Spirit, we are confident and assured that we shall enjoy those blessings. We know that while we are sojourners on earth in this natural body we are absent from the glorious presence of God and the full enjoyment of that for which we have been redeemed. We are not absent from his general presence, which is everywhere (and particularly with his people), but we have not yet entered into our inheritance (1 Peter 1:3-5).

v.7. Our lives, conduct and expectations are regulated by our firm conviction and belief concerning God's mercies and grace to us in Jesus Christ. We see nothing here (by the eye of sense) but misery, sin and death. Faith is spoken of as seeing. 'He that seeth the Son . . . ' We see with the God-given eye of the soul which looks to Christ for all things.

v.8. **'We are confident** of our future happiness and quite **willing** to depart out of this world **and to be present with the Lord'** (Phil. 1:23, 24). Those who are born from above, whose hearts and treasures are above, whose affection is set on things above, inwardly desire to depart from this strange country and live above.

v.9. 'We labour actively in the service and kingdom of the Lord, preaching, witnessing and serving, and we labour passively, submitting to his divine providence, that whether living or dying, whether at home in the body or present with the Lord, we may be accepted in the Beloved.' This is the one concern, the one desire of the renewed heart — to win Christ and be found in him (Phil. 3:8-11).

v.10. All sons of Adam must appear before the judgement seat of Christ (Heb. 9:27). All judgement is committed to the

Son (John 5:22). All judgement is relative to the Son (Rom. 2:16). Men and women who have no interest in Christ, who have not the righteousness of Christ, shall give account of and stand responsible for every secret and open sin. Those who believe on Christ have no sin, therefore no condemnation (Rom. 8:1). Our sins have been both judged and put away in our Lord's sacrifice (Heb. 10:12-17).

Constrained by his love

2 Corinthians 5 : 11-17

v.11. 'Being confident that there shall be a great and terrible judgement of the Lord, before which all must appear (Heb. 9:27), the Lord Jesus himself being the Judge (v.10, John 5:22), at which men shall give account for all that they have thought, said and done in the flesh, **we persuade men** to venture on Christ and believe on him to the saving of their souls. Salvation is only by Christ, who is both able and willing to save the chief of sinners (Heb. 7:25). If a man is in Christ by faith, there is no judgement nor condemnation awaiting him (Rom. 8:1, 34). If men are not persuaded and do not believe us, God knows our hearts and the sincerity of our mission. He knows that we labour for his glory and the good of men. I hope that our faithfulness and honesty are known to you also.'

v.12. The apostle is not praising himself nor commending himself to them, nor does he defend the sincerity of his ministry for their sakes, for they knew him. But he writes these things that they might have a reply for those false apostles and prophets who reproached Paul and gloried in outward show, in circumcision, in learning, in appearance only and who knew nothing about heart conviction, repentance and faith (Rom. 10:9, 10; Luke 16:15; Gal. 6:12-14).

v.13. Paul's zeal and enthusiasm concerning Christ and the gospel of God's grace led many of his adversaries to call him a fanatic, even a madman (Acts 26:24). He tells them that his great zeal and diligence were for the glory of God and the good of the church. 'Whether we be mad, as some say, preaching with great ardour and forcefulness, or whether we be calm and lowly, it is to promote God's glory and your eternal good' (1 Cor. 10:31; Col. 3:17).

v.14. All ministers of Christ and all believers in the Lord Jesus are under the sweetest and strongest constraint to do what they do. They are motivated by **'the love of Christ'** – his love for them and their love for him. It is not fear of hell, desire for reward, nor concern for acceptance that excite believers to their duty, but Christ's eternal love, which led him to redeem them by his life and death, and the love of God which is shed abroad in their hearts (John 21:17; 1 John 4:19). His love for us is the chief motive, for we know that if he died for us, then we were all dead in trespasses and sins (Eph. 2:1). If we had not been dead spiritually, he would not have had to die. Also, if he died for us, we died in him – to the world, to the claims and curse of the law and to ourselves (Gal. 6:14).

v.15. How will men whom Christ loved and for whom Christ died live, labour and conduct themselves? Certainly not to themselves to serve their own profit, honour and ambitions, nor to the flesh to fulfil its lusts and cravings, nor to the world which hates Christ, but to him who died for them and rose again (1 Cor. 6:19, 20). The end of Christ's sacrifice was to redeem us from sin and make us holy (Eph. 1:3-5; Titus 2:14). It is unreasonable to suggest that a person chosen by the Father, redeemed by the Son and regenerated by the Spirit will disregard the commandments of his Lord and live a self-centred, sinful and worldly life.

v.16. The word 'know' in this verse means to approve, acknowledge, or esteem. Paul is saying that he values no man from a human point of view, in terms of natural standards.

Whether a man be a descendant of Abraham, circumcised, learned, rich, gifted, or weak, he regards no man with respect to any fleshly consideration. Christ has taken away all distinctions of the flesh and brought us into a spiritual kingdom (Col. 3:10, 11). Christ was once a man, walked perfectly upon this earth and we did esteem him as such, but we have other thoughts and apprehensions of him now. He is our exalted Saviour and Redeemer, whose kingdom is not of this world. We do not make images and pictures of Christ as a man and use them in worship, but we love and worship him in spirit and truth (Phil. 3:3);

v. 17. **'If any person is in Christ,'** not in religion, in the church, or in moral reformation, but *in Christ,* by faith in Christ, by a new birth wrought in the soul by the Spirit of God, in Christ through electing love, redeeming grace and a living union, he is **'a new creature'** (Gal. 6:15). This new creation describes a creation work, not of man but of God (Eph. 2:8-10; Col. 3:10). It is a new nature, a new man and a new principle of grace and holiness, which was not there before and is distinct from the old nature, the old man, with which we are born in the flesh (John 3:5, 6; 1:12, 13). **'Old things are passed away'** — the old way of life, which loves and serves the flesh, the old legal righteousness and religion, old companions and acquaintances, old desires for riches, honour and human philosophies, and old foolish thoughts of God, self and future glory. The new man thinks and acts from new principles, new rules, with new goals and objectives and in a new fellowship. He has a new commandment of love, a new name, a new song in his mouth, even praise to God, a new and living way opened by the blood of Christ, and an inheritance in the new heavens and new earth. In the new creation absolutely nothing of the flesh is needed, used, nor continued. Our Lord said, 'Behold, I make all things new.'

All things are of God

2 Corinthians 5 : 18-21

There are only four verses in this section, but if, by the grace
of God, a person can lay hold of the things taught in these
verses, he will have a foundation which will not be shaken, a
sure hope in Christ Jesus and the greatest comfort in every trial.

v.18. **'And all things are of God.'** Paul probably referred to
the preceding statement: 'If any man be in Christ, he is a new
creature,' for this complete change which is wrought in conversion is certainly not of ourselves, but of God (John 1:12, 13).
We have a new name, a new heart, a new nature, new principles
and a new family, which are all of grace by the power of God.
But on a wider scale all things are of God – all things in
creation, in providence, in redemption and in the world to
come. He is the first cause of all things! There may be second
and third causes and instruments used by God to accomplish
his purpose (Acts 4:27, 28), but he works his will in heaven and
earth and gives it to whomsoever he will. **'He hath reconciled
us to himself by Jesus Christ.'** Those who were enemies by
birth, nature and choice are now made friends and sons.
Reconciliation indicates a quarrel or separation, and sin is
responsible for that separation. 'Your sins have separated you
from your God.' The law of God is violated, the justice of God
must punish the guilty and the holiness of God will not permit
acceptance or fellowship. But God is not only willing to be
reconciled, he has appointed his Son the Mediator of reconciliation (1 Tim. 2:5). He set forth his only begotten Son in his
purpose and decree to be our representative, our righteousness,
our sin-offering and our atonement (Gal. 4:4, 5) that by his
obedience before the law and by his suffering and death the
law might be honoured, justice satisfied and peace made

between God and the elect. He reconciled us to himself, as
being the party offended, whose law was broken, whose justice
required and demanded satisfaction (Rom. 3:19-26). And he
'hath given to us the ministry of reconciliation', which is the
gospel. By the inspiration of God, the Scriptures were written
(2 Tim. 3:16, 17) which contain the word of reconciliation,
showing that peace and eternal life are in Christ. God also
sends forth his ministers to preach the gospel of mercy and
grace in Christ (Rom. 10:13-15; 2 Tim. 1:8-11; Mark 16:15,16).
This ministry of reconciliation is God-given.

v.19.   **'God was in Christ reconciling the world unto himself.'**
This phrase declares what is the ministry of reconciliation, its
author, its means, its subjects and its consequences. Christ is
God (John 1:1-3; Acts 20:28). In the person of Christ, God
was actually providing himself a lamb, a ransom and an atonement. He did not charge our sins to us but to Christ, having
made Christ to be sin for us (Isa. 53:4-6, 11,12; 1 Peter 2:24).
The word 'world' does not mean that Christ effectually bore
the sins of every person and reconciled every son of Adam to
God by his death. If this were true, no one would finally be
lost. He reconciled the world in the sense that he redeemed a
people out of every tribe, kindred and nation — not of the
Jews only. John Owen said, 'If Christ died for all of the sins of
all men, then all men will be saved; if he died for some of the
sins of all men, then no one will be saved; but if he died for all
of the sins of some men, then some men will be eternally saved.'
This message of substitution and satisfaction by the obedience
and sufferings of Christ has been committed to faithful ministers
of the gospel. We dare to preach it and dare not preach any
other message (Gal. 1:8, 9; 1 Cor. 9:16). Inasmuch as Christ is
our righteousness, God does not call upon us to produce
a righteousness, but to receive his righteousness by faith.
Inasmuch as Christ is our Surety and Substitute, God will not
require satisfaction from us but accepts us in the Beloved
(Eph. 1:6, 7).

v.20. Since God has reconciled his sheep by Christ and has given to his ministers the gospel of reconciliation, then they are certainly the **'ambassadors'**, or representatives, **'for Christ'**. They come sent of him, empowered by him and speaking for him. To hear a true servant of Christ speaking by his Spirit in keeping with his Word is to hear Christ (1 John 4:6). The minister of the gospel speaks in the name of Christ, for the glory of Christ and for our eternal good. His message is that God is reconciled in Christ; Christ died for sinners; there is peace and life to be had through faith in Christ: **'Be ye reconciled to God.'** God is reconciled to us in Christ, but before regeneration and conversion we are still at war with God. Our natural mind is enmity, not subject to God, loving darkness and hating light (1 Cor. 2:14; Rom. 8:7). This is the message of God's ambassador: 'God is reconciled; lay down your arms of rebellion, kiss the Son and be reconciled to God.'

v.21. Christ our Lord had no sin, knew no sin and did no sin. He was perfect before the law of God (1 Peter 2:22; Heb. 4:15). Our sins were reckoned to him. He was identified and numbered with the transgressors and, though he personally had no sin, yet by imputation he was the world's greatest sinner and was dealt with as such and died under the wrath of God (Gal. 3:13; Heb. 9:28; Rom. 8:32). All of this was done that we might be made the righteousness of God in Christ and, by our identification and oneness with Christ, justified. Christ, who knew no sin, was made sin for us that we, who have no righteousness, might be made righteous before God in him (Rom. 10:1-4). With his spotless garments on, we are as holy as his Son (Isa. 45:24). Someone said, 'The gospel can be summed up in two words — *substitution* and *satisfaction*.' Christ, as our Substitute, made full and complete satisfaction for us before God's holy law and righteous justice. In him we are wholly sanctified, completely justified and eternally saved.

The ministry of the gospel

2 Corinthians 6 : 1-10

v.1.   The ministry of the gospel of Christ is a work in which every believer is engaged, whether in preaching, teaching, praying, giving, or witnessing. It is a work which requires perseverance, faithfulness and diligence. We are not in competition, but work together in unity with one common goal — the glory of God (Phil. 1:14-18). However, the meaning here is that we are fellow labourers with Christ. He is the Chief Shepherd; we are under him. He is the Master; we are servants (1 Cor. 3:5-9). Redemption is his work alone ('Salvation is of the Lord'); yet there is a ministerial part which lies in witnessing (Acts 1:8), preaching (Mark 16:15, 16) and teaching (Eph. 4:11-14). In this regard we are **'workers together with him'**. 'We beseech you to receive the gospel we preach; believe it, embrace it and walk therein.' For to hear the gospel, or to be exposed to it, or only to give lip service to it, or to profess to believe it and then turn back is to receive it **'in vain'**! (Heb. 10:38, 39; 2 Peter 2:20-22.)

v.2.   This is a quotation from Isaiah 49:7, 8, and these are words spoken by the Father to Christ! **'I have heard thee.'** He heard him when he stood as our eternal Surety, the Lamb slain from the beginning; he heard him in his priestly prayer recorded in John 17; he heard him in the garden, on the cross and now at his right hand interceding for us. **'In a time accepted,'** or in a time of peace and good will from the Father to men, for God was pleased in the fulness of his own time to send Christ to this world (Gal. 4:4, 5; 1 Tim. 1:15). **'In the day of salvation have I succoured thee.'** While Christ was on this earth working out the salvation of his people by his obedience, suffering and death, he was helped, strengthened and empowered by the

Father through the Holy Spirit. Paul cries, **'Behold,'** before each sentence in order to get their undivided attention. **'Now is the accepted time.'** It is the time of God's mercy and grace to men in Christ. **'Now is the day of salvation.'** The work is done, righteousness is brought in and God is reconciled in Christ. God has purposed, promised and pictured this day throughout the Old Testament. It is all fulfilled in Christ (Heb. 3:6-12).

v.3. To **'give no offence'** is to avoid actions, words, habits and conduct that might be a stumbling-block to others and hinder the success of the gospel preached. The words can be a general precept to all believers, as in 1 Corinthians 10:31-33, or addressed especially to ministers. There are persons who are awaiting all opportunities to reproach the gospel and discredit the ministry of the Word. Let us not give them reason to do so. The next verse seems to bear out the fact that Paul is speaking to ministers of the gospel.

vv.4, 5. It is not only essential that a minister avoid words and actions that might be a stumbling-block and an offence to others, but that he should actively, by all means and ways, prove and show himself to be a true and faithful preacher of the gospel. This is done through **'patience'**, under trials sent by God without murmuring, being gentle and kind in dealing with the infirmities of men and waiting on the Lord to accomplish his purpose. **'In afflictions'** let him be an example to the flock. Let him depend on God to supply his **'necessities'**, for they who preach the gospel are to live by the gospel (Phil. 4:19; Gen. 14:22, 23). Even the minister must endure **'distresses'**, both in body and mind, not knowing what to do nor which way to go (Ps. 37:5). Let him show courage and faith under persecution for the gospel, even in **stripes** (2 Cor. 11:23, 24), in **prison** or bonds for Christ's sake and in **tumults** or uproars and opposition from the people. It is essential that ministers show themselves to be his servants in constant **labour**. God will not own nor bless laziness. A true minister will be known for **watchfulness**, guarding the pulpit and assembly from error of doctrine or spirit, and he will be faithful in **fastings**, whether voluntary or involuntary!

v. 6. The apostle in the preceding verses exhorts ministers to show themselves to be such by way of life and conduct; he now deals with the inward or unseen attitude and spiritual behaviour. If any believers demonstrate **'pureness'** of motive, doctrine and heart, it should be those who teach others. Their **'knowledge'** of the Scriptures and the mysteries of grace and their wisdom in leading God's people come by prayer and study (2 Tim. 2:15; Acts 6:4). The minister must not easily be provoked to anger but by **'longsuffering'**, patience and **'kindness'** must demonstrate the Spirit of Christ. Who is sufficient for these things? Who is able to produce such ideals? None in themselves; but by **the Holy Ghost** and by genuine, **unfeigned love** for Christ and his sheep it is possible.

v. 7. True servants of Christ are also revealed by preaching **'the word of truth'**, the gospel of our Lord Jesus (1 John 4:1-3; Isa. 8:20). They are known by **'the power of God'** accompanying their preaching (1 Thess. 1:5, 6). **'The armour of righteousness'** probably refers to the whole armour of God, as in Ephesians 6:13-17, or especially to the shield of faith in the left hand and the sword of the Spirit in the right.

vv. 8-10. The ministers of the gospel must expect to meet with many different alterations of their circumstances and conditions in this world. They will not be treated, received, nor regarded in the same way by all. They will be loved by some and hated by others. It will be a great evidence of their integrity and faith to behave properly under whatever conditions (Phil. 4:11-13). The apostle met with **honour and dishonour, good reports and evil reports.** He was a **'true'** minister, yet counted by some to be a **'deceiver'**. He was **'unknown'** and unrecognized by most men, but **'well known'** to believers. He was a **dying** man, yet in Christ alive evermore; **'chastened'** by God and men, but not yet given over to death. Like his Lord, the minister is a man of great **sorrow** (Rom. 9:1, 2) over his sin

and the unbelief of others, **'yet always rejoicing'** in the Lord
(Phil. 4:4). It is generally the lot of God's preachers to be
'poor' in this world, but they are the instruments of grace to
'make many rich' spiritually. They have left all to follow
Christ and, therefore, have little or **'nothing'**; but in Christ
they **'possess all things'** pertaining to true life!

Be not unequally yoked together

2 Corinthians 6 : 11-18

v.11. The apostle, having dealt at length with those who
teach, preach and minister the Word of God, exhorting them
to fulfil their ministry, to walk in integrity of life (inwardly
and outwardly), to preach the Word of truth in the power of
the Spirit (all of which he encourages by his own example),
now addresses the whole congregation saying, **'My mouth is
open to you**, to speak freely and openly to you all the counsel
of God (Acts 20:20, 27) and to deal with you faithfully and
plainly. **My heart is enlarged.** I speak openly and plainly to
you because I love you! This strong love for you is what opens
my mouth toward you, for I desire your eternal good.'

v.12. 'I have no difficulty finding room in my heart for all
of you; the trouble is with you. Because of outside influence,
doubts concerning my office and authority and the fact that I
have had to rebuke and correct you for various errors, you
cannot find room in your hearts to love and accept me and my
words' (Gal. 4:16).

v.13. 'Now, by way of return, grant to me the **same rec-
ompense**; repay me with affection; let love be returned for love.
I speak to you as children.' As a father should love his children,
so children should love their father. 'Open wide your hearts to
me as I have opened my heart to you' (1 John 4:7-11).

v.14. **'Be not unequally yoked together with unbelievers.'**
This metaphor is taken from horses or oxen which, being
joined together by a common yoke, must walk and pull
together in the same direction and with the same goal or have
serious problems. Believers and unbelievers do not have the
same principles, natures, nor goals. They cannot walk together
in harmony because they are not agreed on the vital issues of
life, sin, salvation, God's glory and the gospel (Amos 3:3).
Therefore, the believer is unwise who marries an unbeliever
(1 Cor. 7:39), who forms a business partnership with an
unbeliever, who seeks social fellowship and companionship
with unbelievers, who attempts to worship or conduct religious
projects with unbelievers. This is not to be understood as
forbidding any contact with unbelievers in civil society,
conversation, or vocation and trade. If that were true, the
believer would have to leave the world. Also, God put us in the
world as salt and light (Matt. 5:13-16) to witness to all men
and to be an example of his grace, even to those who despise
his name. But to seek an unnecessary alliance and partnership
with one who does not know nor love our Master is foolish,
for what fellowship, companionship and agreement can
righteousness have with unrighteousness? What an absurdity to
think of joining together for comfortable communion darkness
and light, or fire and water! (1 Cor. 10:20, 21; Eph. 5:5-11).

v.15. What harmony can there possibly be between Christ
and the devil? The word **'Belial'** is only used this one time in
the New Testament but very often in the Old Testament and
signifies a very wicked person. Most agree that the reference
here is to Satan. Christ, who dwells in us and we in him, has no
fellowship nor agreement with Satan; therefore, how can we
enjoy unnecessary communion with those who manifest
themselves to be children of the devil? Christ Jesus is our life,
our part and portion; the infidel's part and portion are sin, self
and eternal damnation. Therefore, what do we share in common
that would give us any common ground for communion?

v.16. The argument for believers to quit the company of wicked persons, to separate from them and to avoid being joined unequally with them in unnecessary communion is further enforced by asking, **'What agreement can there be between a temple of God and idols?'** We are certainly the temple of God; for God said, **'I will dwell in them, and walk in them, and I will be their God, and they shall be my people'** (1 Cor. 3:16; Eph. 2:21,22). 'We are **the temple of the living God.'** Idols have no life but are dead things and are representatives of dead men. What agreement or place can life have with or for death? We can no more walk with the living God and find joy and comfort in communion with unbelievers than we can bring dead idols into the temple of the living God! The apostle is not just setting forth the rules and laws concerning unnecessary communion with unbelievers. He is wondering why the believer would seek such alliances and what possible agreement or communion could come of these partnerships! They have nothing in common.

vv.17, 18. Paul does something here that is done in other places in the New Testament. He quotes the Old Testament, not word for word but keeping to the true teaching; in the same quotation he uses another passage (Isa. 52:11; Jer. 31:1, 9). Israel was a special, chosen nation (Deut. 7:6-8) and so were commanded to separate themselves from idols and idol worshippers, from heathen people and their evil ways. The believer is chosen of God, loved, redeemed and called to a life of righteousness; therefore, he ought to and will separate himself from superstition and will-worship in the matters of the soul. He will separate himself from the evil customs and manners of the world, conducting himself as a child of the King. He will separate himself from wicked and immoral persons, not wishing to keep company with them in their sins nor to be exposed to their evil by association. He is not our Father because we separate ourselves from worldly associates and associations, for he is our Father by grace and adoption by his own will in Christ, but he will care for us as a father cares for his children in their every need (Matt. 6:31-33).

Perfecting holiness in the fear of God

2 Corinthians 7 : 1-7

v.1. 'Dearly beloved, since we have the great promises of
God in Christ (2 Cor. 1:20) (*adoption,* God is our Father and
we are his children; *justification,* we are righteous, redeemed
and sanctified (1 Cor. 1:30); *glorification,* we shall be like
Christ and reign with him for ever (Rom. 8:16-18)) let us
cleanse ourselves from everything that would defile body and
spirit.' By the grace of God (1 Cor. 15:10), through the Word
of God (Ps. 119:9-11), with the aid of God's Spirit, let us keep
ourselves clean, not only from fleshly corruption such as
intemperance, drunkenness, profanity, dishonesty, sexual
impurity and idolatry, but also from error of spirit such as
pride, envy, covetousness, malice, evil thoughts and self-
righteousness. 'Perfecting holiness in the fear of the Lord.'
By holiness is not meant the work of perfect sanctification of
the believer before God, for that is wholly the work of Christ,
who is our sanctification and righteousness (Heb. 10:14;
Rom. 3:19-22; 10:3, 4). But this is holiness of life, walk,
conduct and conversation to which we are called and which
is the mark and evidence of a true believer (2 Cor. 5:17;
Eph. 4:21-24). This walk of obedience is motivated not only
by God's love for us and our love for him (2 Cor. 5:14, 15)
but 'in the fear of the Lord' (Prov. 3:7; 16:6). The fear of the
Lord for a believer is not slavish fear, or a fear of wrath and
hell, but a reverential affection as a child for a father. The fear
of the Lord arises from awe, trust, respect and dependence
upon him, and a view to his glory and approval (2 Cor. 5:9).

v.2. 'Open your hearts to us as the ministers of Christ,' Paul
writes. 'Receive us and love us as we love you; for we have not
wronged you, we have corrupted no one by our doctrine, and

we have not cheated nor taken advantage of you.' He is saying that he had done nothing to forfeit their esteem and goodwill (1 Cor. 2:1, 2; Acts 20:20, 27, 33). He could not understand their alienation of heart when he had done nothing to deserve it, but rather had given himself for their eternal good (2 Tim. 2:9, 10).

v.3.   Paul did not call attention to their faults and infirmities only to condemn, reproach, or expose them, but because he loved them (Gal. 6:1, 2; 2 Tim. 2:24, 25). He said, 'You are in my heart and you will remain there; neither death nor life shall change that love nor destroy our fellowship' (John 13:34, 35).

v.4.   **'Great is my liberty of speech toward you.** I open my mouth to you and speak freely even of your faults,' for this is the sign of true friendship and love (Prov. 27:6). We are more reserved and on guard with those who are not close to us. **'Great is my glorying** (or boasting) **of you** to others. I rejoice in your faith, your love and your liberality. **I am filled with comfort**, especially with the coming of Titus and the report he brought concerning your state. In spite of the persecution and tribulation we endure for preaching the gospel, my heart is comforted and I am overflowing with joy because of the grace of God manifested in you and other believers' (1 Thess. 5:16-18).

vv.5, 6.   The apostle met with trouble and persecution in Macedonia from without (that is, from the Gentiles and religious Jews) and from within the church, being troubled by false prophets and unfaithfulness among believers, as well as within his own heart (1 Cor. 2:3-5). The road of faith is not an easy road. The believer is subject to all of the trials brought upon men by Adam's fall (Gen. 3:17-19) and in addition to these he will be hated, oppressed and persecuted for the sake of the gospel (2 Tim. 3:11, 12; Matt. 10:34-39). 'Nevertheless God, who comforts, refreshes, encourages and gives strength to those who are depressed and troubled, comforted me.' Paul is careful to give the glory and praise to God, who is our

Comforter. Though the Lord chastens his people, puts them through great trial and suffering for their good and the fulfilment of his purpose, and though he allows the enemy to try them, as in the case of Job, he never leaves them, never forsakes them but gives them grace and strength to sustain and comfort them (Heb. 13:5; 2 Cor. 12:9; 1 Cor. 10:13). The visit of his brother, Titus, brought Paul great comfort. God is pleased to comfort and strengthen his people in various ways, sometimes by his Word, by his special providence, or by encouragement and fellowship of other believers. But whatever the instrumental cause of joy and comfort, God is the principal cause — he comforts and is our comfort!

v. 7.   Paul was glad to see Titus. However, it was not just his visit that rejoiced the heart of Paul, but the news that he brought. Titus had visited the church at Corinth and had been received with respect and kindness. Titus was greatly encouraged by what he found at Corinth in regard to the things Paul sought to correct by his first epistle — the divisions, the incestuous affair, going to law before unbelievers, disorders at the Lord's Table and misuse of gifts. Titus told Paul of the earnest desire of the church to do the will of God, of their mourning over the sins among them, of their fervent love for Paul and desire to carry out his instructions. This good news rejoiced the heart of the apostle and abundantly exceeded his troubles and afflictions. Nothing rejoices the heart of a minister or a true disciple of Christ more than a good report from others who name the name of Christ (2 John 4; 3 John 3, 4).

Godly sorrow worketh repentance

2 Corinthians 7 : 8-16

v. 8.   The apostle refers to his first epistle to the Corinthians. He had to deal with so many errors of the spirit and the flesh

that had risen in the church that he was sure he had offended
some, grieved others and caused all to be shaken somewhat. He
did not regret writing the letter, for he wrote under divine
inspiration (2 Tim. 3:16), but he regretted the sorrow it
caused. However, that sorrow was only for a little time, for it
led them to repent and correct the errors of which Paul wrote.

v. 9. Paul did not rejoice in their sorrow and grief. No one
can be glad when a brother weeps and is afflicted, even under
the chastening hand of the Lord. But Paul rejoiced in the
effect and results of this experience. Their sorrow led them to
acknowledge their error, to repent toward God and to correct
these abuses of which he wrote. **'Ye were made sorry after a
godly manner'** — that is, their sorrow was of the right kind.
They had not just offended Paul and wronged one another,
but their sin was against God (Ps. 51:3, 4; Acts 5:4). We may
grieve and wound others by our evil conduct and words, but
we sin against God; therefore, true repentance is toward God
and is born of love for God and a desire to do his will. The
goodness of God leads us to repentance. The church suffered
no loss nor harm by what Paul did; rather they gained, because
they repented and corrected matters.

v. 10. These words prove that Christians and churches suffer
no harm, but rather profit by rebuke and correction from
faithful ministers (2 Tim. 4:1, 2). **'Godly sorrow,'** which is a
work of his grace and Spirit, which springs not from fear of
hell and damnation, but from a love for God and grief over
offending him and which looks to Christ in faith for grace and
mercy, leads to salvation and deliverance from evil. Repentance
and faith are inseparable. You cannot have one without the
other. They are like a sheet of paper — there must be two sides
(Acts 20:21). No man has ever believed on Christ without
repentance, and no man will repent apart from true faith in
the Lord Jesus. True repentance will never bring regret, only
rejoicing. **'The sorrow of the world worketh death.'** Esau was
sorry that he lost his birthright, not that he had sinned against
God. All men are sorry when they lose worldly riches, honour,

comfort and reputation, but their sorrow has nothing to do
with their relationship toward God, therefore, it results not in
true repentance, nor faith, nor forgiveness, only death upon
death. True repentance has to do with my relationship with
God, not with this world and its influence (Isa. 55:6, 7).

v.11. Godly sorrow, which works repentance and leads to
deliverance, produces many evidences of the sincerity and
genuineness of it (1 Thess. 1:4, 5, 9). 'What carefulness', to
correct our behaviour before God and to avoid future offences
in this area. 'What **clearing of yourselves,**' not by denying our
guilt and sins, but by confessing them and seeking forgiveness
(1 John 1:9). 'What indignation,' not against God because of
his holiness and law, nor against God's servant for pointing out
our sins, but against ourselves for our folly and our rebellion
(Job 42:5, 6). 'What fear,' not of hell and damnation, but of
God, of incurring his displeasure and of bringing reproach on
Christ (Prov. 1:7; 16:6). 'What vehement desire' to honour
God, to right that which is wrong and to live for the glory of
Christ in this present evil world (Phil. 3:10-14). 'What zeal' for
God and his glory, for the testimony of the gospel and for the
unity and holiness of the church. God forbid that we should
be the occasion for stumbling on the part of one of his sheep
or the occasion for the gospel's being ridiculed by outsiders
(2 Sam. 12:14). 'What revenge,' not against persons in a
private way, for that belongs to God, but against sin and
disobedience, whether found in us or others. This may refer
especially to discipline exercised in the matter of incest found
in 1 Corinthians 5:1-5. In that matter they acted in accordance
with Paul's counsel and cleared themselves by dealing firmly
with the offender.

v.12. Paul declared in this verse that he did not enter into
the problem of the incestuous person for the guilty man's sake
only (though he needed to be disciplined, corrected and
restored to obedience), nor for the sake of the father who had
been wronged, but for the welfare and good of the whole
church, lest the church suffer for permitting such a scandal to

continue. His chief concern was for the glory of God and the good of Christ's church.

v. 13.   What comfort and encouragement Paul received when he learned that the church at Corinth had grieved over their errors, repented toward God and corrected the abuses he had exposed in his letter! True believers grieve over sin and faults, not only in themselves, but in others, and are overjoyed when matters are corrected. They restore the fallen with great joy (Luke 15:10; Gal. 6:1, 2). Paul was especially delighted at the joy of Titus, for he was able to give Paul a good report of the church when he came to visit (2 Cor. 7:6, 7). Believers weep with those who weep and are comforted with one another's comforts.

v. 14.   Evidently Paul had boasted to Titus of the faith, liberality and devotion to him which the church at Corinth had demonstrated. They had not disappointed him, nor proved his words to be false. Titus came to him with a report from the church which confirmed all of the good things he had said of them. Love enjoys a good report and always grieves over any sin (1 Cor. 13:6, 7).

v. 15.   'The heart of Titus goes out to you more abundantly than ever as he recalls and reports to me how submissive you were to his teaching and leadership (Heb. 13:7, 17). You received him and his words with humility and respect.'

v. 16.   The apostle rejoices that he could write and speak to them with confidence that they would hearken to his exhortations in the future as in the past. He may be saying this partly to commend them and partly to pave the way for what he has to say in the next chapter concerning giving.

Abound in this grace also

2 Corinthians 8 : 1-11

In this chapter the apostle praises the churches of Macedonia
for their liberality and generous spirit in the matter of giving,
and he uses their example to encourage the Corinthians to
abound in this grace of giving. Actually, who should give, how
we should give, how much we should give and to whom we
should give form the main theme of the next two chapters of
this epistle.

v.1.   'Brethren, I want to tell you more about the grace,
favour and spiritual blessings of God which have been bestowed
upon the churches of Macedonia, arousing in them love for
others and the desire to give alms and aid to those in need.'
The phrase **'to wit'** means to inform, make known, or to give
knowledge of a thing. Their liberality was the result of the
grace of God in them, for his grace is the fountain of all the
good that is in us or done by us at any time (1 Cor. 15:10;
Eph. 4:32). These churches were Philippi, Thessalonica, Berea
and others.

v.2.   Although these churches were under great persecution
from Jews and pagans, although they had endured great trials
and were in deep poverty, this did not keep them from taking
up a collection and sending gifts to their needy brethren in
other places. They had little themselves but freely gave
generously of what they had (Mark 12:41-44).

v.3.   Two things the apostle points out concerning the
generosity of these churches.
   1. They gave according to their ability and even beyond
what they were able to give — they gave sacrificially.

2. They did it voluntarily and willingly. They were not told to give or how much to give, but rather gave freely and cheerfully, motivated by a love for Christ and the brethren.

v.4. They brought what they had collected among themselves to the apostles and begged them to take the responsibility of distributing these gifts to believers who were in need.

v.5. The apostle expected something from them, even in their condition of poverty and affliction, but what they gave was far beyond his expectation. Here is the reason for their faith and generosity — they first gave themselves to the Lord, to the care of his providence, trusting him to provide for them and resting in his care (Phil. 4:19). Then they gave themselves and what they had to the servants of Christ to be directed and used according to the will of God (Ps. 37:23-25).

v.6. Paul instructed Titus to go to the church at Corinth and receive alms and assistance for those in need. Evidently Titus had dealt with this matter of giving when he was with them before, but the work was not completed, so Paul urged Titus, through the example of the Macedonians, to go to Corinth and encourage among them the grace of giving.

v.7. The church of Corinth excelled and abounded in every grace, according to Paul. He commended their 'faith', by which they had received the Lord Jesus and for which they had courageously stood (1 Cor. 15:1, 2), their 'utterance' or speech, by which they preached the gospel even in other languages, their 'knowledge' of God, Christ and the truth of the gospel, their 'diligence' in discharging their duties to God and men and their 'love' for him and the ministers of the Word. 'See that you abound and excel in the grace of giving as well', for as faith, utterance, knowledge, diligence and love are graces, and the work of God within us, so also are kindness, generosity and liberality. None of these can be exercised properly without the Spirit of God (Gal. 5:22).

vv. 8, 9. 'I am not commanding you to give,' nor does God give a commandment fixing certain sums and times when believers are to give. The Lord has certainly revealed his will concerning giving. There is to be a willing mind (v.12); everyone is to have a part (v.13); and that part is to be as God has prospered or enabled them (1 Cor. 16:2). But Paul seeks to motivate them by three things: by pointing out the example of other believers, by urging them to prove the sincerity of their love to Christ and others (James 2:15-17), and by the example of our Lord Jesus Christ — our Lord gave all for us. Through his love, kindness and grace, he, who was rich beyond description, became so very poor so that by his poverty we might have every spiritual need abundantly supplied. 'Let this mind be also in you which was in Christ' (Phil. 2:5-9). How can we, who are loved in such a way, not also love? How can we, who are the recipients of such grace and mercy, not be gracious and merciful to others?

v. 10. 'It is then my counsel and advice, and it is profitable and fitting for you, to complete this work which you willingly began a year ago.' A good beginning and a willing mind are good, but not enough. We must persevere and do it. Words and good intentions are fine, but the doing of it is essential (1 John 3:18).

v. 11. 'Now, therefore, finish what you began. You showed before that you had the will to help those in need; now perform the doing of it according to your ability or as God has prospered you. Give out of that which you have, be it little or great. No man is expected to give that which he does not have.'

First - a willing mind

2 Corinthians 8 : 12-24

v.12. In the matter of giving, the motive and spirit in which
we give are of greater importance than the amount. There
must *first* be a willing mind. If what we give springs from a
generous, cheerful and willing heart, it is accepted of God,
whether it be little or much, for the Lord does not require of
us that which is not in our power to give. The widow's mite
and a cup of cold water given willingly for the glory of God
are well-pleasing to God (Phil. 4:18).

vv.13, 14. The apostle's meaning is that the burden of the
collection or offering should not be carried by some while
others are excused from giving, but that everyone should give
according to his ability (1 Cor. 16:1, 2). Also, the meaning is
that there should be an equality between givers and receivers —
share and share alike. 'At the present time your brethren are in
need and your gifts will supply that need. At another time their
surplus may be given to supply your want' (Acts 2:44, 45).

v.15. This is a quotation from Exodus 16:17,18 and refers
to the manna which God gave for food in the wilderness. Each
morning it was gathered by the people, by some more, by
others less; yet when it was measured, every man had his omer
and no more. The man who gathered much shared with those
who gathered less, and every need was met. If we are blessed
of God to have an abundance of material blessings, he surely
intends us to share with those who have less strength, ability,
or blessing. This does not excuse nor justify laziness and an
unwillingness to work (2 Thess. 3:10). The true believer does
not look upon giving for the preaching of the gospel and the
relief of the needy as a duty, but as a privilege and a blessing

(Acts 20:35). What we give is not really ours but the Lord's. We are but his stewards and servants (1 Chron. 29:12-14).

vv.16, 17,   Paul requested of Titus that he go to Corinth for the purpose of receiving a collection and to assist them in the matter of giving, but God had already laid the matter on the heart of Titus, and though he made the journey at the suggestion of the older apostle, he willingly did so of his own accord. How blessed is the service of the Lord when it is motivated by his grace and done with a willing heart!

vv.18, 19.   Who this brother was is difficult to say. Some have suggested Luke, Barnabas, Silas, Apollos, or Mark, but one thing is clear, he was a brother who faithfully preached the gospel. Also, he was one chosen by the churches to travel as Paul's companion when he carried a large gift for distribution among the needy. On that occasion, as now, Paul's end was the glory of God and to show his readiness to help others.

vv.20, 21.   Paul is careful to have another brother, designated by the church, with him when he is entrusted with gifts and money for distribution. This is not only to provide things honest in the sight of God, but also in the sight of men. Paul would not handle so large a gift alone lest someone should think that he had applied it to his own use or did not distribute it to those for whom it was intended. Paul could be trusted and he certainly trusted Titus, but he did not know what men might say; he therefore takes along or sends along a witness. Let us be careful to pattern our methods in the handling of collections in the same way (2 Cor. 13:1).

v.22.   Paul mentions sending another brother of good report and faithful service along with them.

v.23.   This verse contains Paul's words of recommendation for Titus and the brethren sent to Corinth to make up their collection and gifts for the needy in other places. In the matter of preaching the gospel Paul, on another occasion, discounted

letters of recommendation, saying that the gospel he preached
and the fruits of his ministry were his letter of recommendation
(2 Cor. 3:1-3). But in the matter of handling finances and
receiving to hand large gifts to be taken to other places, Paul
feels it necessary to express his personal confidence in these
men and to assure the church at Corinth that they can be
trusted fully. 'As for Titus, he is my partner and fellow-helper,
and the other two brethren are chosen messengers of the
churches and a credit and glory to our Lord.'

v.24.   'Therefore, when they come your way, receive them
and show to them (before all) the reality and truth of your
love to Christ, to others and to me. Show also that I have good
reason for boasting about and being proud of you.'

God loveth a cheerful giver

2 Corinthians 9 : 1-15

In this chapter Paul continues his teachings on the subject of
giving, with directions concerning the acceptable way and
manner in which this grace should be performed, as well as
some fresh arguments and encouragements for being diligent in
the grace of giving.

v.1.   Paul thought it unnecessary to say much more to them
about the offering or collection to be received for the poor
and needy. He had covered the subject quite well and had sent
three brethren to them, who knew the subject well and were
capable of instructing them.

v.2.   He also was well acquainted with their willingness and
had boasted of their zeal and enthusiasm in this matter to the
churches of Macedonia. He told these other churches that
Corinth was prepared last year to get on with this business,

and this stimulated the majority of them to do likewise.

v.3. Yet, knowing the frailty and changeableness of human nature, knowing the power of the enemy, knowing that men are prone to grow cold and indifferent and knowing the need for constant encouragement and teaching in spiritual matters, Paul sends the three brethren on their mission to Corinth (Matt. 26:41; Heb. 3:13, 14). 'I want you not only to be ready in heart, but in hand, **lest our boasting of you be in vain.**'

v.4. Paul writes, 'If I should come there and some of the brethren from Macedonia (to whom I had spoken so proudly of your charitable work) should come with me and find that you had done nothing, only talked about giving and sharing, I would be ashamed, to say nothing of your own embarrassment.'

v.5. 'Therefore, I thought it necessary to send Titus and the brethren to you before I came down, that they might make arrangements in advance for this gift of yours which has been so much spoken of, that it may be received and ready. It must be a willing and generous gift, not a matter of extortion nor given reluctantly' (Exod. 35:5; 1 Chron. 29:9).

v.6. A covetous person may think when he gives money, goods and alms to others that the amount given may be charged to loss, but not so! It is no more loss than the seed planted by a farmer is lost. The farmer must turn loose of the seed, give it up and bury it in faith that God will multiply it according to his will. So it is with giving. We willingly part with our gifts generously, sharing that which God has placed in our hands, knowing that he will supply our needs according to his will. The farmer must also be free and generous with the seed, for the more seed sown, the greater the harvest. If we give sparingly and grudgingly, we will reap the same, but if we are moved by God's grace so that blessings may come to others and we give generously, we shall also reap bountifully.

v.7. 'Let every person (not just the prosperous or a few)

give as he has been led of the Spirit, as he has made up his own
mind, as he has determined in his own heart and, of course, in
proportion as God has blessed him. Let him give cheerfully
and joyfully, not reluctantly nor out of duty and necessity, for
God loves, takes pleasure in and blesses a willing, cheerful giver'
(Prov. 22:9).

v. 8.   Generous men do not lose by giving to others, for God
is able to make all sorts of gifts (both spiritual and temporal)
come their way (James 1:17; Phil. 4:19). 'As you are enabled
by God and moved in your hearts to give, the Lord will provide
for you in all things and will also enable you to abound in
other good works.'

vv. 9, 10.   This is a quotation from Psalm 112:9 and declares
that the benevolent person who is merciful, generous and gives
to others shall be blessed of God, and the fruit, influence and
results of his work and example will live for ever. 'God, who
provides seed for the sower and bread for food, is both able
and willing to supply you with whatever you need and bless
your acts of kindness for his glory and the eternal good of
those to whom you minister.' It is God who gives us a willing
heart, who supplies us with means to give and who uses the
gifts we give for his glory.

v. 11.   Works of charity and grace do not impoverish us, but
rather are means to enrich us. Can a man lose by doing that
which pleases God and that of which our Lord himself is the
great example? (2 Cor. 8:9.) Give liberally with humility and
simplicity, and God will enrich you in all things and your
generosity administered to others will bring forth much
thanksgiving to God.

v. 12.   The two great ends of every believer's life are the glory
of God and the good of others. As Paul and the apostles
disperse the gifts to needy people, both of these ends are
served. The needs of many are met and the people glorify God
and give thanks to him.

v.13. Most believe that this collection and these gifts were for the poor believers in Jerusalem and, being sent by these Gentile churches, would only cause them to glorify God the more and be strong proof of the Gentiles' subjection to, and love for, the gospel of Christ. True Christianity is a submission to the gospel of Christ, is evidenced by labours of love and works of charity and results in praise and glory to our God (Matt. 5:16).

v.14. 'Those whose needs are supplied by your generosity will respond and make the best return they are able, by loving you, longing for your presence and fellowship and praying for you.'

v.15. **'Thanks be unto God for his unspeakable gift,** our Lord Jesus Christ — the giver of every gift, the fountain of all blessings and the only Saviour of sinners.' This gift is indescribable, inexpressible and beyond telling.

The weapons of our warfare

2 Corinthians 10 : 1-7

Paul met with much opposition at Corinth from false preachers and teachers. He had many enemies there who boasted in themselves and refuted both Paul and his doctrine. They envied him and did all that they could to undermine him and lessen his influence. They represented him as a harsh, mean-spirited man and insinuated that he had neither the authority nor the courage which he claimed. In this chapter he vindicates himself and arms the Corinthians against these self-seekers.

v.1. Paul's enemies evidently had charged him with being meek, gentle and humble when he was present with them, but when he was away, he wrote forceful, bold and condemning letters. Is not this the example of our Lord, who never compromised the truth about men, yet was meek and gentle, kind and patient toward all? When we find ourselves inclined to be rough or angry with men, let us think of the gentleness of Christ, be sensible of our own infirmities and yet be bold in our quest for godliness in spirit and deed (2 Tim. 2:24, 25; 4:1, 2).

v. 2. He urges them to hear him, follow him as he follows Christ and submit to his teaching, that he might not, when he comes among them, have to use that power and authority given him by Christ (Heb. 13:7, 17). He does not want to deal boldly with them all in general, as he plans to deal with some who have accused him of acting according to the flesh (1 Cor. 4:21). These false preachers accused Paul of the very thing of which they were guilty, that of seeking his own worldly interest and secular advantage and employing craftiness and fleshly wisdom and methods to accomplish it (2 Cor. 1:12).

v. 3. There is a difference in walking *in* the flesh and walking *after* the flesh or warring after the flesh (Rom. 8:1, 4-6). Every believer walks in the flesh, in the body, in a state of imperfection, attended with many weaknesses and infirmities, but he does not walk after the flesh in that his fleshly appetite, desires and pride are not his end, goal and objective. The glory of God and a godly way of life are the desires of every renewed heart (Phil. 3:10-14). Nor does the believer war after the flesh! The work of the ministry and the Christian life are spiritual warfare (1 Tim. 1:18; 6:12; 2 Tim. 2:3, 4), but this battle is not fought upon fleshly principles, using fleshly methods, nor yet for fleshly honour and glory. We seek his glory and the true salvation of sinners (Jer. 9:23, 24; 1 Cor. 10:31).

v. 4. The goal of the Christian ministry is not carnal but spiritual. We seek not lip-service from men but heart love to Christ. It is not our goal to bring men to outward morality and reformation alone, but that they might be new creatures in Christ, delivered from the kingdom of evil to become bond-

slaves of Jesus Christ, motivated to holiness and godliness by
new and spiritual inward principles. Therefore, our weapons
and methods are not carnal nor of the flesh, but spiritual
(John 6:63). The strongholds of Satan are ignorance, prejudice,
vain imagination, carnal wisdom and beloved lusts. These can
only be pulled down by the mighty Spirit of God, bestowing
grace and life through the gospel. Our weapons in this warfare
are the sword of the Spirit (the Word of God), prayer, gifts of
ministering and love to Christ and his people (Eph. 6:11-15).
We dare not depend on anything the flesh can produce. If God
does not work in us and through us, we labour in vain.

v.5.   The preaching of the gospel of Christ is the power of
God to destroy the strongholds of Satan in the minds and
hearts of men, casting down every proud thought of self-
righteousness, every high and lofty reasoning of human
wisdom, as opposed to his revealed truth, every reliance on
our works or deeds which might be a rival to his grace in
Christ, every high and haughty look or feeling of confidence in
what we were or have become, and bringing us, mind and heart,
thought and attitude, into a full and complete dependence
upon and obedience to Christ Jesus (1 Cor. 1:26-31; Col.
2:9, 10). Repentance is the gift of God; faith is the gift of
God; eternal life is the gift of God. All that we are, know and
shall ever be are gifts of God and the work of God in us
through, by and for the glory of our Lord Jesus (Eph. 2:8-10).
We have nothing of which to boast in the flesh (1 Cor. 4:7).
What we do is in response to what he has done in us and for us
(1 John 4:19).

v.6.   The apostle refers here to church censure and excommunication to be exercised upon those who depart from the
gospel of God's grace. Paul would not tolerate another gospel,
the dishonouring of the name of Christ, nor a disorderly walk
among church members. These offenders are to be dealt with
by the church, not hastily, but prayerfully, patiently and only
after our own submission and obedience to Christ are secured
and complete. Church censure and excommunication are

painful but necessary where the honour of Christ, the glory of God, the well-being of the church and the testimony of the gospel are concerned.

v. 7. 'Do you look upon and judge men by outward appearance?' (1 Sam. 16:7; Luke 16:15.) Are you so weak in spiritual wisdom that you judge men by their faces, their outward appearance, their claims and their voices and words? A man may appear to be gracious and not have the principle of grace in his heart. A man may appear to be learned in the Scriptures and not know Christ. Don't be misled by the outward appearance of some; redemption is a heart work. 'If any among you is confident that he has an interest in Christ, is redeemed by his blood and is a believer, let him reflect and remind himself that on the same basis (which is the mercy and grace of God in the person and work of Christ) we, too, have a saving interest in him.' We must not think that none belong to Christ but ourselves. By the grace of God we are what we are, and his grace is effectual to save even those who differ from us.

He that glorieth, let him glory in the Lord

2 Corinthians 10 : 8-18

Paul defends his ministry against the false preachers who despised him, opposed him and judged him by appearance. Spurgeon once said, 'The best way to expose a crooked stick is to lay a straight stick down beside it.' Every generation is plagued with false preachers and religious hucksters (Matt. 7:15; 2 Peter 2:1-3).

v. 8. When God calls a man to be a prophet, an apostle, an evangelist, or a pastor (Eph. 4:11-13), he is pleased to give that man gifts, ability and certain authority (2 Cor. 13:10; Heb. 13:7, 17). This power is not for the destruction, oppression,

nor discomfort of the flock, but for their edification, to
promote their faith, holiness, comfort and eternal salvation.
Paul was not ashamed to speak of, nor to exercise this authority.
Let all who have office or authority in the church remember
that with authority goes responsibility to edify and unify, not
destroy.

vv. 9, 10.   This was the charge against Paul which came from
his enemies and false preachers: 'When he is absent and writes
to the church, his letters are weighty, powerful, forceful and
demanding of obedience to God, yet when he is present, he
does not impress men with his appearance, grandeur and
forceful oratory, but rather his bodily presence is small,
frail and old, and his speech is humble, without impressive
persuasion and contemptible to those who are looking for a
hero to worship.' What they thought to be an insult to Paul
was a strong recommendation of his true call of God (1 Cor.
15:9, 10; Eph. 3:8; 1 Tim. 1:15; Phil. 3:3). God never intended
us to be impressed with men, to adore men, nor to be obsessed
with preachers, but to worship only Christ (2 Cor. 4:7; 1 Cor.
2:4, 5).

v. 11.   Paul declares, 'But those who judge by appearance
only and think, because I walk in humility before God and
men, that I am not an apostle with due authority, let those
people realize that what I say in letters, I will put into deeds
when I am present.' There comes a time to deal forcefully with
rebellion and disobedience (1 Cor. 5:4, 5).

v. 12.   Paul refuses to evaluate either himself or his ministry
by the method used by these teachers of false religion to
commend themselves. They were pleased with themselves,
prided themselves on their righteousness and estimated their
value in the kingdom of God by comparing themselves with
themselves and others. Paul denounces this as unwise (Isa.
65:5; Luke 16:15; 18:9). If we have any grace, gifts, or ability,
they are given and sustained by God, and even at our best we
are all altogether vanity in his sight (1 Cor. 4:7; Ps. 39:5).

Feeding our egos by comparing ourselves with others is foolish.

v. 13.   They had among them men who boasted immeasurably,
or beyond the gifts which they had. Paul had a better rule for
his conduct: not to boast of any gifts, graces, or authority
other than those God had obviously given to him and not to
go beyond his God-given commission as to duties and place of
service. His authority and ministry included the Corinthians.
What an important lesson for all believers! Each member of
the body has a place and a service to perform. Learn what it is
and seek not to be otherwise nor to envy another (1 Cor.
12:12-18).

v. 14.   Paul declares that he had not gone beyond the bounds
set for him by the purpose and providence of God in edifying
and instructing the church at Corinth, for he was indeed sent
by God to them (Acts 18:1, 9-11). Another evidence of his
being in the will of God by ministering among them was that
God had blessed his labours with success (Matt. 7:16).

vv. 15, 16.   When Paul rejoiced in the Corinthians as his
children and converts (whom he had begotten through the
gospel of Christ), he was not taking credit for the labours of
other men, as did these false preachers, who, when they came
to Corinth, found a church planted with many believers. Yet
these men claimed the Corinthians as their own, belittled Paul,
and troubled the church with their errors. His hope concerning
this church was that as they were grounded in truth and
grown in Spirit, his field of labour would be enlarged greatly,
and both he and they would be the instruments of God to
preach the gospel in regions beyond, where the name of Christ
was not known. He was not interested in interfering with, nor
boasting in, work already done by others before he came on
the scene.

v. 17.   But none of us really has anything in which to glory
(Jer. 9:23, 24; 1 Cor. 1:29-31), neither Paul who planted nor
Apollos who watered, for it is God who gives the increase

(1 Cor. 3:5-7). We have no reason to glory in ourselves nor in our works, but only to thank, praise and give glory to God, who is pleased to use human vessels to accomplish his divine purpose.

v.18.   It is not the man who praises and commends himself who is approved and accepted, but it is the person whom the Lord enables, approves and commends (Prov. 27:2). Self-commendation means nothing; rather than lifting us, it really lowers us in the estimation of true believers and is nauseous to God.

The simplicity that is in Christ

2 Corinthians 11 : 1-8

In this chapter Paul continues to expose the false teachers in the churches who sought to lessen his influence and who were preaching another gospel. He calls them false apostles, deceitful workers and ministers of Satan. In denouncing these false apostles, he feels it necessary to defend his apostleship and his ministry among the Corinthians and to call their attention to his dedication to the gospel of Christ and his own sufferings in the service of Christ.

v.1.   Matthew Henry wrote, 'As much against the grain as it is with a proud man to acknowledge his infirmities, so much is it against the grain with a humble man to speak in his own praise.' What Paul here calls **'my folly'** is his effort to speak in his own defence and his own commendation. This is foolishness unless a man has a good reason. Paul knew that he had a good reason, which was to preserve these believers from being corrupted by false preachers who had crept in among them. He knew that he was the Lord's messenger to the Gentiles (Acts 9:15, 16), and he knew the tragic results if these men

were successful in discrediting him, so he begs them to bear
with him as he speaks of himself and the ministry God has
given him.

v. 2. Jealousy is a feeling within a person which demands
exclusive loyalty and resents a rival or competitor for the
beloved's affections or attention. Paul's jealousy toward the
Corinthians was not so much on his account nor with a selfish
motive, for he called it a **'godly jealousy'**. He was instrumental
in bringing them to Christ, to believe on him and to be joined
with him in union as a husband and wife are one (Eph. 5:23-25).
He desired to present them to Christ, and only to Christ, as a
chaste virgin comes to her husband, single in their love to him,
sincere and upright in their worship of him and faithful, not
having their minds and hearts distracted in any way from him
by these false teachers of law and self-righteousness (Gal.
6:12-14).

v. 3. This godly jealousy in Paul was a mixture of love and
fear. He loved them, deeply desired their eternal good and
feared lest they should be corrupted by these deceivers. Satan
used the serpent to seduce Eve from her obedience to God
(Gen. 3:1-6). He was crafty, skilful and deceptive, as are those
men who do his bidding under the guise of righteousness
(vv.13-15). Believers are complete in Christ, who, of God, is
made unto us wisdom, righteousness, sanctification and
redemption. Satan's one goal is to corrupt the mind and turn
the heart away from this singleness or simplicity of Christ. It
matters not to him if it be law, morality, tradition, ceremony,
or whatever (good or bad), just so as there is a rival for Christ's
pre-eminence and his sufficiency. Christ plus anything in
redemption is not the gospel of God's glory and grace (Col.
2:9, 10) but is another gospel (Gal. 1:6, 7). The foundation of
the great Reformation was the Scriptures alone, grace alone
and Christ alone. Nothing needs to, or should be added to
these (Rom. 5:1, 2; 2 Cor. 5:21). In Christ believers are
perfectly justified and righteous before the Father.

v.4. Some interpret this to mean that 'If some particular
preacher comes to you preaching another Jesus, another spirit,
or another gospel which is more for the glory of God and the
comfort of believers than the Christ, the Spirit, and the gospel
which Paul preached, you might well follow and honour him.'
I cannot imagine Paul even supposing such a ridiculous thing,
since there is *one* Lord, *one* Spirit and *one* gospel. But Paul
was troubled because he knew that these false apostles were
preaching another Jesus, another spirit and another gospel,
which was a mixture of works and grace and of law and faith,
and he was greatly concerned lest the people hear these men
and be persuaded by them to turn from the simplicity of
Christ (1 Tim. 2:5; Eph. 4:4-6). How prone the flesh is to
listen to the wrong voice and reject the true messenger!
(John 5:43.)

v.5. 'You would do well to bear with me, for I am not one
degree inferior to those who were apostles before me (2 Cor.
12:11), such as Peter, James and John.' This he says in answer
to those who questioned his apostleship, since he was not with
the original twelve (Gal. 1:17; Rom. 11:13), and also to show
how foolish the Corinthians were to prefer these false preachers
before him.

v.6. The apostle Paul was intelligent, highly educated, skilful
and at home among kings or common people (Acts 22:3;
26:24). However, he did not in his public ministry use philosophy, human wisdom, flowery words and oratory, but spoke
in the plain, popular style of the common people to whom he
ministered (1 Cor. 2:1-5). 'Though I seem to some to be
simple in my speech (2 Cor. 10:10), yet I am well taught in
the knowledge of Christ and his Word' (Gal. 1:11, 12). Too
often flowery words and sermons are used to cover a deficiency
in the knowledge of Christ. Even our blessed Lord spoke to
the people in parables, stories and illustrations which they
understood in their heads, if not in their hearts. 'God has been
pleased to own my ministry among you,' he declared, 'and
clearly reveal to you, by your own conversion and growth in

grace, that he sent me, and my gospel is his gospel.'

vv. 7, 8. It seems that some in this church highly valued the false apostles, who compromised the gospel, flaunted themselves in pride and authority and made merchandise of the people, and they treated with contempt this true servant of Christ, who had freely and humbly preached the gospel to them. He asks, 'Where did I offend you? Was it because I came to you in fear and trembling, without pride and arrogance, using a popular tongue suited to the common people, working with my own hands as a tent-maker, that I might not be a burden to you? Rather than being offended, you ought to be grateful. I took wages of other churches and accepted more than their share of my support to preach to you' (1 Cor. 9:13-15). What fools we are to judge things spiritual by outward appearance and claims of men! (2 Cor. 10:7, 18.)

Speaking in defence of the ministry of God's servant

2 Corinthians 11 : 9-21

v. 9. There are always those who are eager to charge the ministry or churches with covetousness, greed and 'being in religion for what they can get out of it materially'. When Paul ministered in Corinth for nearly two years, he deliberately took nothing from them in order to dispel any doubts concerning his one objective – to preach the gospel for the glory of God and the salvation of sinners. He made tents for a living (Acts 18:1-3) and received help from the brethren in Macedonia. He had never been a burden to them and resolved never to be.

vv. 10-12. Mature believers are taught by the Spirit and the Word of God that those who study, preach and labour in the gospel are to live by the gospel and are to be supported comfortably by those to whom they minister (1 Cor. 9:11-14;

Gal. 6:6). Paul was determined to take nothing from the
Corinthians, but to labour at his own expense, as he did in
Thessalonica (1 Thess. 2:5-9). He informed them of the reason
for this conduct and the reason why he boasted openly of the
fact that he preached without charge to them. It was not
because he did not love them, nor was unwilling to receive
tokens of their love and friendship, but it was to avoid giving
his enemies occasion to accuse him of preaching to enrich
himself. This put the false apostles, whether rich or poor, on
the spot. They claimed to be equal or superior to Paul, so, in
the light of his willingness to be abased or to abound, to labour
with his hands and to take nothing from men, let us see if they
will work on the same terms that Paul worked — only for the
glory of God and the eternal good of men.

v.13.   Unfortunately, there have always been and are now
many **'false apostles'** (Matt. 7:15, 16; 2 Peter 2:1-3; 1 John 4:1),
who pretend to be sent of God, but are not. They are **'deceitful
workers'**, who not only lie about their call and serve themselves
and not Christ, but they handle the Word of God deceitfully
(2 Cor. 4:2). They never were apostles of Christ; they only
pretend to be.

v.14.   This is no marvel nor strange thing; for Satan himself,
in order to deceive men, appears as a messenger of light, truth
and righteousness. Pretending friendship, he designs ruin;
under a cloak of religion and morality, he promotes evil; under
a show of partial truth, he introduces great error, idolatry and
superstition. Too many people look for Satan only in bars,
nightclubs and dens of open evil. This is more of his deception.
He does his most effective work in the pulpit, in religion,
promoting self-righteousness, tradition and substituting any
hope other than Christ's righteousness and effectual sin-
offering, which is the sinner's only hope (Heb. 10:14-18).

v.15.   Since Satan, in order to receive men, pretends to be
what he is not, so those who are his ministers, who seek their
own profit and not the glory of God or men's salvation, will

pretend to be what they are not. They pretend to be ministers of righteousness, but if you examine carefully, you will find that the righteousness they preach is not the righteousness of Christ but the righteousness of law, human works and deeds of religion (Matt. 5:20; Rom. 3:19-23; 10:1-4). Their end will correspond with their deeds, or their reward at last will be according to their works.

vv. 16, 17. Referring back to what he said in verse 1, Paul expresses the hope that no man would think him to be unwise and guilty of foolishness in commending himself and his ministry to them and vindicating himself against the false apostles. If they did not think him to be a fool, then he asked them to bear with him in this folly; for he felt it necessary for the sake of the gospel and for the good of the church not to allow these insinuations against him to go unchallenged. He did not have a special command of God to defend or commend himself. God's servants are taught to be humble and to commit their ways unto the Lord, but Paul felt that the glory of God and the best interests of the church would be served by his speaking plainly about his credentials, even if some thought it to be foolish boasting.

v. 18. It is a fact that most men glory with respect to things external, such as their birth and families, their riches and possessions, their beauty and strength, or their education and influence. The apostle says, 'I will glory also, not in these things, but in the grace of God in me and the power and gifts of God upon me' (Jer. 9:23,24; Phil. 3:4-9). Paul detested this sort of thing, for he kept saying, 'I speak as a fool' (vv. 21, 23), but he felt it necessary to call attention to his integrity in the Word and put to silence these false preachers.

vv. 19, 20. 'Notwithstanding all of your so-called wisdom' (1 Cor. 4:9, 10) (the Corinthians prided themselves on both their natural and spiritual wisdom), 'you gladly bear with these false preachers, these proud boasters who bring you again under the bondage of the law and works, who exploit you, who take your money and possessions, who proudly exalt themselves over you and who belittle you like a slap in the face' (Gal. 2:4; 4:9). All of this was taken in good part by many so that they rejected Paul and came under the influence of these false preachers.

v.21.   Paul says, 'I reply to the reproaches they bring against me, claiming that I am weak and contemptible, for indeed I am less than the least of all, the chief of sinners, but not in my doctrine or in the ministry I have among you, for where any man may be bold, I am bold! I speak foolishly as does anyone who speaks to his own praise, but I must tell you the truth that you may know God has sent me.'

If I must needs glory

2 Corinthians 11 : 22-33

For the glory of God, for the sake of the gospel, for the good of the church at Corinth and to expose the false prophets for what they were, Paul continues to vindicate himself and to defend his ministry and his message of justification by faith (Rom. 3:28). They said that he was weak and contemptible, that his speech was rude and they urged the people to reject Paul and follow them. So Paul was forced to expose them (vv.12-15) and defend himself (vv.16-18).

v.22.   **'Are they Hebrews? So am I.'** Evidently these false preachers were Jews who sought to bring into this Gentile church their traditions and impose on the Corinthians the ceremonies and requirements of the law (Col. 2:16, 17; Gal. 3:1-3; 5:1-6; Rom. 10:4). They boasted that they should be heard because they were Hebrews, descendants from Jacob (Israelites) and sons of Abraham (John 8:33). Paul declared that his credentials in this regard matched theirs (Phil. 3:3-7).

v.23. 'Are they ministers of Christ?' Paul might have denied
that they were true ministers of Christ, since they did not
preach Christ, they put down the true apostle to the Gentiles
and they sought their own things, not the things of Christ nor
the good of the church. This a minister sent by Christ would
not do! But Paul chose not to do battle with them on this
point (by pointing out their inconsistencies and errors) but
rather to show in himself the spirit, sufferings, motives and
dedication to Christ and the church which are characteristic
of a genuine apostle and preacher. He regretted having to
commend himself ('I speak as a fool'), feeling that it would be
misunderstood (v.16; Prov. 27:1, 2), but there was a reason for
it — to stop the mouths of these vain boasters. He was more
than a minister of the gospel; he was an apostle who laboured
more and suffered more then even the other eleven apostles.
Therefore, he was far superior to these who found fault with
him.

1. 'In labours more abundant.' He travelled more, preached
and wrote more, established more churches and even worked
with his own hands. He was a tireless evangelist.

2. 'In stripes above measure.' He suffered more for the
gospel (being beaten, whipped and unmercifully afflicted) than
any other.

3. 'In prisons more frequent.' Who spent more time in
prison for the sake of the gospel than Paul? Certainly not these
false apostles!

4. 'In deaths oft.' He was always in danger of death. The
afflictions, evils and dangers to which he was constantly
exposed threatened death (2 Cor. 1:8-10).

vv.24-27. In proof of his love for Christ, his dedication to
the gospel of God's glory and grace and the fact that God had
counted him faithful in the ministry of the Word, the apostle
reveals some of the things he had suffered for the testimony of
God. Paul was the apostle of the Gentiles and for that reason
was hated of the Jews and among the Gentiles he also met
with great persecution. Five times he was whipped by the Jews
(Deut. 25:1-3); three times he was beaten with rods (Acts

16:19-23); once he was stoned (Acts 14:19); three times he
suffered shipwreck (we read of only one — Acts 27:18-44).
'A night and a day I have been in the deep' may refer (as some
say) to a dungeon, but most likely it refers to being adrift on
the sea after a shipwreck. If he journeyed by land or by sea,
he was always in danger, for it seemed that everyone wanted
to silence his voice. Satan used every means, from bandits to
false brethren in the church, to add to the toil and hardship of
Paul. He suffered hunger, thirst, cold, exposure and lack of
clothing. When we are tempted to complain of our lot in life,
it would do well for us to review these verses and consider how
little we have suffered for what we believe (Heb. 12:4).

v.28.   Besides those afflictions and trials which were brought
upon his flesh and body (his outward man) by people who had
no relation to Christ or to the church (1 Cor. 5:12, 13), the
apostle was burdened in heart and mind with the care of all
the churches. He was not an ordinary pastor with the responsibility of preaching to and overseeing one church, but he was
the Lord's apostle in these earliest days of the conversion of
pagan Gentiles, who had to be taught the ways of Christ, and
the conversion of traditional, legalistic Jews, who had to be
taught that Christ was the fulfilment and the end of the
Mosaic law. Not having the completed New Testament as their
rule and guide, all of these early churches looked to Paul and
the inspired apostles for guidance, instruction and correction.

v.29.   'Who is weak that I do not feel his weakness?' There
was not a weak believer struggling with problems of foods,
days, inner conflicts, or temptation, with whom Paul did not
sympathize (Rom. 12:15). There was not an offended believer,
hurt and wounded by what he did or said or by the words and
actions of someone else, that did not cause Paul pain and grief
until the cause of the offence was removed. This oneness with,
and compassion and sympathy for, members of the body of
Christ are not only the minister's responsibility, but should be
the feeling of all believers (1 Cor. 12:25, 26).

vv.30, 31. What Paul says in these verses is that if he must commend himself and if it becomes necessary for him to prove his apostleship and the integrity of his ministry, he will do so, not by pointing to his unusual gifts, such as the different languages he spoke, miracles he had performed, churches he had established, or the great numbers of people who had been saved by his gospel, but he chose to glory in the things he had suffered for his faithfulness to the gospel and to glory in his genuine love and concern for the people of God. He calls on God as his witness that he speaks the truth (Rom. 1:9; 9:1-3).

vv.32, 33. He mentions one incident in the past in which he was in great danger, but God delivered him. This was his first great difficulty and the rest of his life was more of the same (Acts 9:21-25).

My grace is sufficient for thee

2 Corinthians 12 : 1-9

The apostle Paul continues in this chapter to vindicate himself and his ministry against the false preachers, taking notice of a very remarkable and unusual experience with which God favoured him and of the method God used to keep him humble and to keep him from being exalted. Yet for all this, he chose rather to glory in his infirmities and hardships for the sake of the gospel.

v.1. It is neither comely nor is there anything to be gained by our boasting in our works, our gifts, or our accomplishments (Jer. 9:23, 24), nor would Paul do it except when it was necessary for the glory of God and the overall good of the church. Having spoken of his hardships and great sufferings for Christ, he comes to visions and revelations which God gave to him. His conversion was the result of what he called a 'heavenly vision' (Acts 26:19). At Troas a vision appeared to him, in which a man of Macedonia called him there to preach (Acts 16:9). The Lord spoke to him in a vision, revealing to him that he should remain in Corinth, for God had much people there (Acts 18:9, 10). These visions were for his instruction, direction and encouragement in the ministry of the gospel. We have no need of special visions and voices from heaven, for we have the completed Word of God. All that we need in order to know Christ and have eternal life is revealed by the Holy Spirit through the Word of God (Rom. 10:17; 1 Peter 1:23).

vv. 2, 3. Paul speaks of himself in the third person instead of the first. The men whom God used to write the Scriptures often did this. Verse 7 clearly indicates that he referred to himself. He says, 'I knew a man in Christ,' that all the glory and honour might be to Christ, for no heavenly blessing nor heavenly revelation can come to any man except in, by and for the glory of Christ (Eph. 1:3). Paul was taken up to 'the third heaven', the seat of divine majesty, the abode of holy angels, where the glorified Christ is and where departed believers go following death. In verse 4 he called it 'paradise' (Luke 23:43). Some say the third heaven is above the heaven where the birds fly and above the starry heaven which is adorned with stars and planets. Whether he was taken there in body and spirit, or in spirit only, he did not know — only God knows!

v. 4. Paul did not speak of what he saw there but only of what he heard, calling the language and words unspeakable (either impossible for a man to utter, or impossible for men in the flesh to comprehend, or both). Though they were spoken in the presence of a man, yet they could not be spoken by him! Not that it would be sinful for him to speak these heavenly words, but that it was impossible for him or for any earthly creature to understand, enter into, or participate in this heavenly state until they are changed to his likeness (1 Cor. 15:50, 51). This exposes as falsehood the testimonies of people today who claim to have died and who come back telling what they saw and heard. Heavenly glories are as impossible for the human mind to comprehend and express as music, art and science are above the understanding and communication of a dog. Only glorified people can speak of or understand the true glories of heaven.

v. 5.   In this experience the Lord greatly exalted and honoured Paul, and though he might and did lawfully glory and rejoice in the Lord, who had so highly favoured him, yet he knew that it was not owing to any merit or worthiness found in himself. He found all grace and mercy in Christ and only for the glory of Christ. If he gloried in anything of himself in his present state, it would be in his infirmities and weaknesses, those things which he had suffered for the glory of God. He had been faithful to the gospel even under the most difficult circumstances (2 Tim. 4:5-8).

v. 6.   Again the humility of the apostle shines forth in this verse, for he says, 'Should I have a mind to boast or glory in this unusual experience, I would not be a foolish braggart (as some might interpret it); for I would be telling nothing but the truth — a true account of what really happened. But I forbear, suppress any desire to relate all of the revelations and visions God has given me, lest anyone should take me to be more than I am — a sinner saved by the grace of God' (Eph. 3:7, 8; 1 Tim. 1:15; Rom. 7:24).

v. 7.   God took care of any tendency in Paul to be proud or puffed up over the greatness of his gifts and revelations by giving him a thorn in the flesh. Pride is naturally in every man's heart and believers are not without it; therefore, to prevent this sin, which God hates (Prov. 6:16, 17; 16:18), God gave Paul a thorn in the flesh, a messenger of Satan to harass him. We know that God permitted this affliction; we know that it had to do with Paul's flesh (human nature). Whether it was sickness, weakness, temptation, lust, or appearance, we do not know, but we know that it was a messenger of Satan, or, as God was pleased to put Job in the hands of Satan, he was pleased to allow Paul to be tried sorely and afflicted by the

angel of hell. The plain and evident purpose for this severe trial
in the flesh was to keep Paul from becoming proud, puffed up
and exalted above measure. Instead of being a hindrance, this
thorn was a help to the apostle, as our infirmities, afflictions
and trials are for our eternal good (Rom. 8:28; 1 Peter 1:6, 7).

vv. 8, 9.   Three times in definite, dedicated and sincere prayer,
Paul asked God to deliver him from this affliction, to remove
it from him, but the Lord refused, telling Paul that his grace
was sufficient to support him, strengthen him and uphold him
under any trial or circumstance. Besides, God's strength and
grace are never more glorified or appreciated than when we
realize our own weakness and inability! Therefore, Paul said,
'I will all the more rejoice in and accept my weaknesses and
infirmities, that the power of Christ may rest upon and be
revealed in me' (2 Cor. 4:7).

We seek not yours, but you

2 Corinthians 12 : 10-21

When Paul prayed three times for God to remove the thorn in
his flesh, the answer God gave him was wonderfully satisfactory
to him. **'My grace is sufficient for you,'** to strengthen, comfort
and bear you up under and through whatever trial or affliction
it is my purpose for you to experience (Phil. 4:11-13). The
Lord's strength and grace are more manifest, are more glorified
and are more appreciated in the light of our weaknesses
(Luke 7:47). Paul considered himself to be a weak, feeble,
sinful creature and the power and grace of Christ to be his
refuge, his salvation, his shield and his strength.

v. 10.   **'Therefore,'** he said, **'I take pleasure in the infirmities
of the flesh, in reproaches** from Satan and men, **in the common
necessities** of life (such as hunger, thirst and nakedness),

in persecutions from the enemies of the gospel (whether in the church or out), **in distresses** of mind and heart and for all things that I am called upon to suffer **for Christ's sake; for when I am weak** in myself and aware of my inability and the arm of flesh provides no help, then my Lord strengthens me, meets my need and reveals his grace, and **this is my real strength.'** When we have nothing to say, to contribute, or to find comfort in, we will look to Christ and find that in him are all things! To live, we must die; to be full, we must be emptied; to be rich, we must become poor!

vv.11, 12. Paul declared that in calling attention to his revelations, his office and his sufferings, he felt like a foolish person, for it was against the principle of grace, against his humble spirit and against the truth of divine providence for him to boast (1 Cor. 4:7). But these people forced him to do it by listening to the false preachers and taking sides against Paul. They ought to have spoken in his defence, for he was the instrument of God in their conversion, and he was not one whit behind the greatest apostles in call, gifts, labours, or suffering, though in himself he knew that he was nothing (1 Cor. 3:5-7; 15:9, 10). Indeed, the signs and credentials of a genuine apostle were performed among them by Paul and revealed in wonders and mighty deeds (Rom. 15:16-19; Heb. 2:3, 4).

v.13. 'You have not been neglected, not treated any differently than the churches where Peter or James or the other apostles ministered. You have heard the same gospel, witnessed the same miracles and been enriched in the same spiritual gifts. The only difference is that I took no financial support from you, but provided for my own support by labouring with my hands. If this offended you, I apologize' (2 Cor. 11:7-9).

vv.14, 15. Paul planned to visit them again and lets them know that he was coming to them with the same resolutions, not to be a financial burden to them. His chief reason for this determination was to impress upon them the fact that his only concern was their salvation, their growth in grace and their fellowship in Christ, not material, nor physical, nor personal gain for himself. He looked upon them as his children and, though children ought to help parents who are in need, yet it is the duty of parents to provide for children. He declared that he loved them so exceedingly that he would spend all that he had and be willing to labour and even die for their spiritual welfare, though it seemed that the more he loved them, the less they loved him.

vv. 16, 17. 'You must admit that I did not burden you at all, and the false accusers will admit it also, but they suggest that I was crafty and sly, making use of other persons to get your money, while I professed to preach the gospel freely.' Paul desires them to name even one person of the many messengers he sent their way who had received anything from them for him. Enemies of the gospel seek their own and are not only cruel in their accusations, but usually have no regard for truthfulness.

v. 18. He urged Titus to visit them and sent a brother with him. He asked, 'Did Titus take advantage of you in any way? Did he not act in the same spirit in which I acted and take the same steps, seeking your good and not his own?' God's true ministers all are of the same Spirit. They seek the glory of God and the good of the church, not their own gain, glory, or welfare (1 Tim. 3:1-7).

v. 19. Did Paul speak all these words about his ministry, his labours and his sufferings only to defend himself against false charges, to build himself up in their eyes, or to gain their favour? No! It was for their sake, for their edification, because he loved them, that they might be grounded on the true foundation, the Lord Jesus Christ, built up and established in the faith of the gospel. He spoke in all sincerity, without deceit, before God as one in Christ. He was fearful lest they be led astray by listening to the wrong voice. God speaks through men, but since there are so many false preachers, we must try them and their message (1 John 4:1-3; Rev. 2:2).

vv. 20, 21. Paul closes this chapter by expressing the fear that when he visited them again, he would find things in the church not honouring to Christ and contrary to holiness, such as quarrelling, envy, wrath, strife, selfishness, gossip, pride and disorder. 'If I find you in these things, you will not find me to be so co-operative, but quite severe in my dealings with those who will not repent of their sins and walk in godliness.' This would cause the apostle great distress, grief and sorrow of heart to have his visit concerned with discipline instead of comfort. 'Put away these things from among you and walk together in love and purity, that the name of Christ be not slandered' (Eph. 5:1-4).

Examine yourselves

2 Corinthians 13 : 1-14

v. 1. Some understand the words, **'The third time I am coming to you,'** to mean his one visit to them in person (Acts 18:1, 9-11), his first epistle and now this second epistle. This is probably what he meant, for he called to their attention the law concerning witnesses in any matter (Deut. 19:15). Our Lord also referred to this rule in Matthew 18:15, 16. The gospel he preached, the things he taught, the way of life he had called them unto and the correction and rebukes for their errors had all been established by the Spirit of the Lord in the mouth of two or three witnesses (John 5:31-39; 1 John 5:7, 8). We would do well to use the same rule in all matters before us today.

v. 2. He means that he had in the first epistle faithfully told them of the evils that existed among them (the divisions, false preachers, fornication, going to law with one another, divorce,

misuse of gifts and bad behaviour at the Lord's Table) and had
warned them to correct these errors. Now, being absent, he
writes the second time to the whole congregation, and especially
to the guilty parties, that if these matters are not corrected by
the time he comes to them in person, he will use his powers as
an apostle to deal with the offenders. This was one of the
reasons he had been reluctant to visit them; he wanted his visit
to be pleasant and not tumultuous (2 Cor. 1:23). Those who
love Christ love and enjoy peace and unity. They do not delight
in conflict and division.

v.3.   Some of the members of this church, prompted by false
apostles and teachers, had called into question Paul's authority
(his apostleship) and had suggested that perhaps he did not
speak for God at all. Of all men, these Corinthians had the
least reason to question Paul's ministry, for he had been the
means and instrument God used to bring them to faith in
Christ. Christ's message of grace, spoken through Paul, was
certainly not weak but mighty in them. It was the power of
God unto salvation to them and was attended among them
with signs, wonders and gifts of the Holy Spirit. True converts
are living proof that God speaks through a minister. Those
who make a false profession are the fruits of false prophets
(Matt. 7:15, 16).

v.4.   'Our Lord is not weak but mighty; his gospel is the
power of God unto salvation (Rom. 1:16). His blood is effectual,
his righteousness is sufficient, his Spirit is invincible, and those
whom he has purposed to save will be saved (Ps. 110:3; John
6:37-39; 10:23-30). There was a time when Christ was weak
and was crucified in weakness (Isa. 53:1-3). He was made flesh
and numbered with the transgressors, but by the power of God
he arose and ascended to heaven, where he lives and reigns for
ever. We apostles are weak like he was, and for his sake bearing
reproaches, persecutions and afflictions as he did in the day of
humiliation, but we are strong in Christ (Phil. 4:12, 13) and
through Christ, who enables us to perform the gospel ministry
(2 Cor. 10:3-5).

v. 5. 'Now instead of examining me and seeking proof of Christ's speaking through me, examine yourselves! Determine by the Word of God if you are in the faith of Christ. Don't spend your time proving others but prove yourselves! (2 Peter 1:10, 11). Do you not know your own hearts? If Christ dwells in your hearts by faith, you have become new creatures, his Spirit is within you, his graces and fruit are manifested, his love is shed abroad in your hearts and you have a good hope. If not, you are counterfeits, worthless and rejected.

vv. 6, 7. Paul expresses the hope that the Corinthians would know that he was not counterfeit, rejected of God and a hypocrite. He also prayed to God that they would believe the Word, love Christ and walk in the Spirit of God – not just to make him appear to be something great or even to vindicate his claims, but that they might know and love the Lord Jesus and be redeemed even if his ministry was never accepted and men considered him to be a counterfeit.

v. 8. The gospel is true! God is sovereign! The will of God in covenant mercies and the redemptive work of Jesus Christ shall be victorious! Neither Paul, the Corinthians, nor any man, nor all men, nor the forces of evil can do anything to alter God's purpose or defeat his truth. Whether in obedience or rebellion, we contribute to his greater glory! (Isa. 46:9-11; Acts 4:27, 28; Rom. 9:15-18; Ps. 76:10.)

v. 9. The apostle declares that he was glad to be weak, to be afflicted and to bear reproaches for Christ's sake that the power of Christ might rest upon him and result in their becoming strong in faith and active in the exercises of grace (2 Cor. 12:10; 2 Tim. 2:9, 10). This was his desire above all things that they know Christ and reach maturity in faith (Eph. 4:11-15).

v. 10. Therefore, he wrote this epistle while he was absent from them, that they might set things in order among themselves (Phil. 2:12, 13), that when he did visit them in person he would not be forced to use his apostolic authority and rod which the Lord gave him. The Lord put him in the ministry to edify men, not to destroy and trouble them.

vv.11-14.   The apostolic benediction: 'Brethren, be mature believers, not babes which are always in need of correction and rebuke. Be of good comfort in your trials and afflictions, knowing they are for God's glory and your good (Rom. 8:28). Be united in mind and heart, in purpose and affection. Live together in peace among yourselves and as much as possible with all men, and the God of love and peace will bless and be with you. Greet one another with mutual love and genuine friendship. Don't avoid others and hold grudges but show your love openly. The saints in other places greet you. The grace of the Lord Jesus Christ and the love of God and the communion of the Holy Spirit be with you all' (Num. 6:24-26).

BIBLE CLASS
COMMENTARY SERIES

by
Henry T. Mahan

Notes

Notes

Notes

Notes

Notes

Notes

Notes

Notes

Notes

Notes

Notes

Notes

Notes

Notes

Notes

Notes

Notes

Notes

Notes